THE GREAT COMMISSION

John M. Strohman, J.D.

Published by:
Cross Centered Press
113 Village Drive
Pierre, SD 57501

Softcover ISBN: 978-0-9859949-3-8
Kindle (e-book) ISBN: 978-0-9859949-4-5
E-Pub (e-book) ISBN: 978-0-9859949-5-2

Unless otherwise noted, verses are cited from the *New American Standard Bible* 1977 edition and 1995 update with permission. *The New American Standard Bible®*, Copyright 1960,1962, 1963, 1968, 1971, 1972, 1973, 1975, 1977, 1995 by the The Lockman Foundation.

Some references or portions in this book originate from another work of this author entitled *The Application Commentary of the Gospel of Matthew*. Softcover ISBN: 978-0-9859949-0-7, Kindle ISBN: 978-0-9859949-1-4, E-Pub ISBN 978-0-9859949-2-1.

While efforts have been made to ensure accuracy, if you identify an error in this publication, please send a notice to john@CrossCenteredMissions.org. Please include the page number and sentence, along with your suggested correction.

Chief Editor – Trish Sargent, M.A.

The opinions contained herein are the author's and do not represent another or any institution/organization.

DEDICATION

To my dear family,

I have been blessed by your being alongside while we labored to build the kingdom of God, and not the kingdom of Strohman.

ABOUT THE AUTHOR

 *The most distinguishing feature of the author is that he is a sinner who, in his early youth, was saved from the judgment to come by the grace of God. He continues to recognize his complete reliance on the mercy, forgiveness and grace of Jesus Christ <u>to this very moment</u>.*

* Other matters: John M. Strohman is a graduate of the University of Iowa College of Business and earned his Juris Doctor from the University of South Dakota School of Law. For over two decades he has served as an Assistant Attorney General for the State of South Dakota. As an attorney with 25 years of experience, he has handled a variety of cases, including serving as counsel for more than 150 cases before the South Dakota Supreme Court. John has also held faculty positions as an adjunct professor for Liberty University, South Dakota State University, Northern State University and Colorado Christian University. His teaching experience has spanned both the undergraduate and graduate level. In 2012 he authored *The Application Commentary of the Gospel of Matthew*. He has served on mission boards and is the current chairman of Cross Centered Missions. John and his wife, Sarah, share a passion for equipping young people in Christian service through discipleship, Sunday school, Bible studies and leading short-term mission trips.

Oh yes… and at age 53, he can still do a backflip!

Preface

It is my hope to stir the reader into a serious examination of the true calling on his life. Even Christians can be subject to the influences of the world around them. Some of these influences include the world defining what Christianity is *supposed* to look like. The world's definition requires that Christians be nice, do a few good things, never judge, and keep their mouths closed, unless they are advocating viewpoints that will not offend anyone. The reward for such compliance is worldly acceptance, religious approval and financial contributions.

This book does not simply explore what the world is telling the church to be, it also examines what a growing segment of the visible church is telling the true Church to be. It will examine questions such as whether the Bible really calls us to "preach the gospel at all times, and if necessary, use words." What does it really mean when Jesus said to do it to "the least of these?" Does a person become a true brother of Christ simply because he is poor, hungry, thirsty, sick, imprisoned or lacking adequate clothing? Is it possible to delude yourself into thinking that you are a faithful Christian by doing what you believe are "good works" yet ignore what Jesus has actually commanded you to do? Who gets the glory when good deeds are performed, but the Cross is not proclaimed? Is it possible that many in the church are really modern-day Pharisees who are content to clothe themselves with religious appearances when in reality they are simply "...*holding to a form of godliness, although they have denied its power; avoid such men as these.*" (2 Timothy 3:5)

You are alive today so you still have time to engage in the true Great Commission and finish strong. Let us get started!

[The author does not belabor the reader regarding gender issues with repeated statements of "he or she" in general comments and examples of people. The reasonable reader will recognize that in my general comments, using terms like "mankind" or "he", are obviously meant to include women.]

TABLE OF CONTENTS

THE
FAKE
COMMISSION

CHAPTER 1

SPIRITUAL MALPRACTICE?

> Jesus said *"...Let us go somewhere else to the towns nearby, so that I may preach there also; for that is what I came for."* (Mark 1:38).

Matthew 28:18-20 is a section of scripture that is often referred to as the Great Commission. Why is it called that? Why is it so great? What is a commission? To answer these questions, start by breaking down the definitions of each word. Webster defines (in part) these words as:

> *Great*: "Huge, Predominant, Principal, Main, Noble."[1]

> *Commission*: "(3) a: authority to act for, in behalf of, or in place of another; b: a task or matter entrusted to one as an agent for another...."[2]

So what is the huge, predominant, principle, main and noble task that we have been entrusted to act on behalf of another?

> Matthew 28:18–20: *"And Jesus came up and spoke to them, saying, 'All authority has been given to Me in heaven and on earth. Go therefore and make disciples*

---

[1] *Merriam-Webster Collegiate Dictionary, 11ᵗʰ edn.*

[2] Ibid.

> *of all the nations, baptizing them in the name of the*
> *Father and the Son and the Holy Spirit, teaching them*
> *to observe all that I commanded you; and lo, I am*
> *with you always, even to the end of the age.'"*

How does Webster define (in part) the word *"Fake"*?

> *Fake:* "One that is *not* what it purports to be: a:
> worthless imitation passed off as genuine;
> b: imposter, charlatan; c: a simulated movement in a
> sports contest (as a pretended...or a quick movement
> in one direction before going in another)."[3]

So what is the fake commission? It is pretending to be engaged in a noble task on behalf of another; all the while producing a worthless imitation that was never intended. This book will analyze some of the causes, effects and consequences of the fake commission. It will not end there, suggestions and solutions will also be discussed. The footnotes at the bottom of some pages will be part of that discussion. A number of footnotes will simply identify the source used, while others will expand over a couple of pages for those who desire a more comprehensive explanation of a concept. With this as a roadmap, let us move on to our first example of a well-intentioned solution that goes very bad.

Imagine you are enjoying a beautiful Saturday morning stroll down the sidewalk. Then in a moment, you suddenly feel ill! You stumble and grab at a rickety old wooden fence next to you to steady yourself. A friend driving by sees you, and can tell there is something terribly wrong. He quickly pulls over, puts you in his car and drives you to the hospital.

Once at the hospital, you are whisked into an emergency room. Following right behind you is a gray-haired doctor who has been practicing medicine for over 30 years. He notices you are having trouble breathing and that you are clammy and sweating.

---

[3] Ibid

The doctor looks concerned and quickly asks, "Tell me, how you are feeling?" You grab a couple breaths and say, "I'm nauseated...cold...little dizzy." With your eyes wincing in pain you say, "Doc, I feel this tightness in my chest...and numbness in my arm—bad tingling in my fingers. The grim-faced doctor quickly scans down your arm to your hand and then...breaks out in a smile and says, "I see your problem! You have a large splinter in your finger!" Confident that he can relieve your pain, the doctor grabs the alcohol bottle to clean the finger with the splinter. While focusing on your hand, he does not notice that you are fading in and out of consciousness. He quickly and carefully begins to remove the splinter. Just as he holds up his tweezers in triumph— you collapse... and die of a heart attack.

As an attorney with over 25 years of experience, I will assure you that the doctor committed medical malpractice. Malpractice is defined as "...a dereliction of professional duty or a failure to exercise an ordinary degree of professional skill or learning ...[resulting in] an injurious, negligent, or improper practice."[4] So why was the doctor's conduct malpractice? The answer is simple: When you came into the emergency room and told the doctor you felt clammy, nauseated, dizzy, and had shortness of breath, chest pains and numbness down your arm, your symptoms screamed out that you were having a heart attack! It did not matter that the doctor could *see* your finger had a splinter in it from the wooden fence that you grabbed to steady yourself. It was the *unseen* heart that was the real problem. The doctor's medical textbooks clearly stated that your symptoms represented your true *unseen* condition...you were having a heart attack. The problem is that the doctor became *distracted* by what he could *see* (the splinter). Because he ignored his medical textbooks, his incompetence will surely result in the loss of his license to practice medicine in addition to being sued for malpractice. Clearly the doctor has some huge problems—but not as big as yours; you're gone— forever.

---

[4] *Merriam-Webster Collegiate Dictionary, 11th edn.*

So what is the point of that story? As Christians, we can be tempted to engage in a lethal form of spiritual malpractice. This occurs when we fix our eyes on what we see as the problems in a person's life, instead of trusting the perfect textbook, the Bible, to tell us what the real problem is: (*"...His divine power has granted to us everything pertaining to life and godliness, through the true knowledge of Him...."*) (2 Peter 1:3). This spiritual malpractice manifests itself when we twist the term *mission* to mean a focus on social issues, physical needs, building construction, or denominational promotion. When this happens, we have misdiagnosed the person's true terminal condition.[5] A person's greatest need is not to escape poverty but to *escape the judgment to come.* Like the incompetent doctor, many Christians find it easier (and more rewarding) to focus on the troubles they can *see*, rather than trust what God's Word says is a much more serious, fatal, damning and eternal problem that cannot be seen.

The word of God makes it clear that the *ultimate need* in a person's life is not food, clothing, clean water, healthcare, education or social justice. By far the greatest need in a person's life is to escape the judgment to come. Worldwide, tens of thousands of people enter hell each day having a full stomach and a warm house. Many die in a hospital while receiving the world's

---

[5] Unfortunately, this is not as unusual as one thinks. There are "mission organizations" claiming to be Christian who have either dismissed preaching the true gospel or relegated it to a very insignificant segment while the focus is on physical relief. In exchange, they have received large corporate assistance and their donations have grown. Obviously when you engage the unbelieving world to *help* in ministry, the non-Christian has no interest in the real Jesus. Given enough time, the real Jesus will be removed and thus, by definition, the organization is no longer Christian regardless of its claim. An organization does not get to define what Christianity is—Jesus Christ does. Scripture states that *the church is subject to Christ*, Ephesians 5:24. It also states clearly that *"Christ also is the head of the church, He Himself being the Savior of the body."* (Ephesians 5:23). An organization that claims to be Christian but later denies the real Jesus, is simply exploiting the name of God for money and cloaking itself in the appearances of righteousness. As it says in 2 Timothy 3:5: *"...holding to a form of godliness, although they have denied its power; Avoid such men as these."*

best healthcare. Others die just as tragically, shelterless, starving, and without medical care. The equalizing factor of the rich or poor, privileged or despised, educated or ignorant...is that they all have sinned, and all will die.

The World Health Organization published that "in 2012, an estimated 56 million people died worldwide."[6] This averages to slightly more than 153,424 deaths each day (which mean that *every 30 seconds* approximately *53 people died*).[7] For the 106 people who died one minute ago, it is now irrelevant what their physical condition, social economic status, or education level was. Their most important question is: How many of them a minute ago entered an *eternity* condemned to hell *forever*? Or maybe the more exacting question is how many of the 56 million in 2012 were saved by Jesus Christ and entered eternal life forever? Jesus gives us a hint at the answer in Matthew 7:14 when He used the word *"few"* to describe the number who find life: *"For the gate is small and the way is narrow that leads to life, and there are few who find it."* When you ponder the 56 million who died in 2012, what number comes to your mind when you hear Jesus use the word *few*?

When we speak of eternity we are talking about where you will spend the next 20 billion years—(understanding that 20 billion years merely represents the start of your infinite eternity). Thus it is easy to understand why Jesus makes it clear that one's eternal destiny is infinitely more important than a person's

---

[6] World Health Organization - Media Centre - Fact Sheets. http://www.who.int/mediacentre/factsheets/fs310/en/index2.html

[7] World Health Organization 2012 averaged worldwide death rate 56 million. 56,000,000 deaths in 2012 / 365 days = 153,424.6 deaths each day. There are 86,400 seconds in a day = (24 hours x 60 mins. X 60 seconds). 153,424.6 deaths each day / 86,400 seconds a day = 1.7757 deaths per second. So the number of deaths every 30 seconds: (1.7757 deaths per second. X 30 seconds = 53.271). So on average, every 30 seconds 53 people die and enter eternity.

physical condition, or even the preservation of one's own earthly life!

> Matthew 18:8-9: *"If your hand or your foot causes you to sin cut it off and throw it away. It is better for you to enter life maimed or crippled than to have two hands or two feet and be thrown into eternal fire. [9] And if your eye causes you to sin, gouge it out and throw it away. It is better for you to enter life with one eye than to have two eyes and be thrown into the fire of hell."*

> Luke 12:4-5: *"And I say to you, My friends, do not be afraid of those who kill the body, and after that have no more that they can do. [5] But I will warn you whom to fear: fear the One who after He has killed has authority to cast into hell; yes, I tell you, fear Him!"*

The Bible states that man's spiritually dead condition is the result of his sin against God's law. Jesus did not come to focus on "helping people." He could have stayed in heaven and sent others to help people. His purpose for coming was to be the atonement for our sins and inform people how to be saved by that atonement. *"In Him we have redemption through His blood, the forgiveness of our trespasses, according to the riches of His grace."* (Ephesians 1:7). Jesus said: *"...I must preach the kingdom of God to the other cities also, for I was sent for this purpose."* (Luke 4:43). In the discussion of missions, one should start with a working definition. Real missions should be defined as:

> <u>MISSIONS:</u> It is the true church (with love for God and people) sending out the truly converted to another location or culture (nearby or far away) for the purpose of sharing the gospel of Jesus Christ; making disciples of Jesus Christ; baptizing them in the name of the Father, Son and Holy Spirit; teaching them to obey all that Jesus Christ commands, and doing the good works for the sole glory of God.

Ch. 1: SPIRITUAL MALPRACTICE?

(Footnote 8 below expounds on the definition of missions.[8])

---

[8] <u>True church/truly converted</u>: The ministry is not to function with false converts. Keep an eye out for them because they will show up. Acts 8:21–22: *"You have no part or portion in this matter, for your heart is not right before God. Therefore repent of this wickedness of yours, and pray the Lord that, if possible, the intention of your heart may be forgiven you."* Ephesians 5:5: *"For this you know with certainty, that no immoral or impure person or covetous man, who is an idolater, has an inheritance in the kingdom of Christ and God."*

<u>Love for God and people</u>: Matthew 22:37-40: *"And He said to him, 'You shall love the Lord your God with all your heart, and with all your soul, and with all your mind.' This is the great and foremost commandment. The second is like it, 'You shall love your neighbor as yourself.' On these two commandments depend the whole Law and the Prophets."* Only true love causes us to warn people how to escape the judgment to come and to care about their physical condition. Like a godly king, we should care for others who are weak: Psalm 72:12-14: *"For he will deliver the needy when he cries for help, The afflicted also, and him who has no helper. He will have compassion on the poor and needy, And the lives of the needy he will save. He will rescue their life from oppression and violence, And their blood will be precious in his sight…."*

<u>To another location or culture to preach</u>: Mark 16:15: *"And He said to them, "Go into all the world and preach the gospel to all creation."* <u>Nearby or far away</u>: Acts 1:8: *"…but you will receive power when the Holy Spirit has come upon you; and you shall be My witnesses both in Jerusalem, and in all Judea and Samaria, and even to the remotest part of the earth.""*

<u>Sharing the Gospel of Jesus Christ</u>: Romans 10:14–15: *"How then will they call on Him in whom they have not believed? How will they believe in Him whom they have not heard? And how will they hear without a preacher? How will they preach unless they are sent? Just as it is written, "How beautiful are the feet of those who bring good news of good things!"*

<u>Making disciples, baptizing, and teaching them to obey Jesus</u>: Matthew 28:18–20: *"And Jesus came up and spoke to them, saying, 'All authority has been given to Me in heaven and on earth. "Go therefore and make disciples of all the nations, baptizing them in the name of the Father and the Son and the Holy Spirit, teaching them to observe all that I commanded you; and lo, I am with you always, even to the end of the age.'"*

<u>Good works</u>: If you obey Jesus' commands to love God and your neighbor as described in Matthew 22:37-40, you will share the gospel and engage in the "good works" that God ordained for you to do: Ephesians 2:8–10: *"For by grace you have been saved through faith; and that not of yourselves, it is the gift of God; not as a result of works, so that no one may boast. For we are His workmanship, <u>created in Christ Jesus for good works</u>, which God prepared*

The Biblical model of a mission trip is first and foremost, the proclamation of the gospel. The great missionary of the New Testament, the Apostle Paul, explained it this way:

> **1 Corinthians 15:3–4:** *"For I delivered to you as of <u>first importance</u> what I also received, that <u>Christ died for our sins according to the Scriptures,</u> ⁴and that He was buried, and that <u>He was raised on the third day according to the Scriptures,</u>...."*

Unfortunately, this is not the model used in many modern churches. Every summer, hundreds of churches in this country send their youth groups out on short-term missions to be trained in the fake commission. Many of the fake commission groups engage in a religious version of the "peace corps." They typically start out attending some basic "team building" exercises. Spiritually irrelevant training like—someone stands on a chair and falls backward and is caught by the rest of the group.[9] Then they launch out to engage in a week emphasizing a social endeavor such as cleaning up an area, building a house or helping at a soup kitchen. Let me be clear: It is true that Christians are to be engaged in good works like feeding the poor, providing shelter, advancing education, administering healthcare and visiting *"orphans and widows in their distress"* (James 1:27). These

---

beforehand so that we would walk in them." Holy Spirit-led good works will not result in glorifying you, your organization or even your church denomination—they will glorify God alone. Matthew 5:16: *"Let your light shine before men in such a way that they may see your good works, and <u>glorify your Father who is in heaven.</u>"*

[9] How that exercise builds up a person's faith in the Lord Jesus is still undetermined. I think it is supposed to mean you can trust your life to those going with you; a naive conclusion at best. Psalm 118:8: *"It is better to take refuge in the Lord Than to trust in man."* Instead we should be built up in faith by studying God's Word. Romans 10:17: *"So faith comes from hearing, and hearing by the word of Christ."* Our training should be meaningful (see 1 Corinthians 9:25–27). We are told *"All Scripture is inspired by God and profitable for teaching, for reproof, for correction, <u>for training in righteousness.</u>"* (2 Timothy 3:16)

good works are to *flow out from the act of true evangelism...not serve as a cheap substitute for true evangelism.* True missionary teams are to be trained on how to share the gospel Biblically, so they are able to warn others on how to escape the judgment of their sin.

I am not proposing some theory on this subject. I have trained short-term mission teams for 16 years and have been engaged in evangelism for more than 35 years. The objective of mission teams I have worked with remains the same: preach the gospel *while* doing good works for the glory of God. To accomplish this we first try hard to start with committed Christians. This starting point will offend some people in the church who have godless kids. Often mission trips are greatly hindered because the trip leaders feel pressure to take whoever signs-up (whether they are adults or youth).[10] Remember, the

---

[10] Often someone will tell the mission leader to take a particular person on the mission trip, suggesting that, "it would be good for 'Billy' to have this Christian experience." The problem is the mission leader knows Billy has no interest in the things of God, attends youth group under duress from his parents, and leads others to mock what is taught. I will not take along a "Billy." As attractive as it sounds that you are "reaching out" to Billy, an effective mission team's function is not to spend its time trying to *save* its own team. Billy has his church and youth group to learn about the things of God... if he has any real interest in doing so. If you take Billy along to "fix him" he will end up ridiculing leadership and rebelling against the work. Further, he is not going to effectively share the gospel, because it is not real in his own life. If he is somewhat of a natural leader, he will create other malcontents. Billy will also waste a lot of your time on the trip trying to keep him happy so to minimize his complaints when he gets home to his dad, who is an officer in the church.

Think of it this way: How many professional football teams are composed of players who have never played football and further, do not even like the game as a spectator? Likewise, youth leaders need to free themselves from the pressure of taking everyone who signs up for the mission trip. Do not worry about looking unsuccessful because you have only a group of five solid, committed disciples of the Lord. Yes, some in church leadership will think you are a successful youth leader because you have 112 kids on the mission trip. They conveniently ignore that 85% of them do not manifest any fruit that they are even saved. This is why the fake

work is too serious to take along those who will ultimately undermine it. I am not trying to provide a great "youth group experience" for the kids at the church. Charles Spurgeon addressed this concept when he wrote an article entitled *"Feeding sheep or amusing goats?"* Spurgeon's point is that the church is not responsible to entertain non-believers (or believers for that matter). Next, our mission groups are prepared - trained - equipped to follow the words of Christ and reach out to lost souls with the gospel as the primary purpose of the mission i.e. share

---

commission works so well for most churches. If the mission trip is focused on buildings and social work, Billy and the rest of the unsaved (kids and adults) can conveniently come alongside without as many problems. If the mission work is really focused on the Great Commission, Billy will be a huge problem!

Also, select the adults who will come with you with great care. Do not take an adult who makes it clear to you or the church that he/she is incurring a significant sacrifice by going. Make sure your adults have a true vision for the work. Without a real focus to accomplish the Great Commission, they will be much harder to deal with than any youth. They will hinder the work and create factions while constantly trying to change the vision of the mission.

One last tip: If there is any way possible, I would suggest you: a) pay your own expenses/raise your own support for the mission trip and, b) do not receive a payment for leading the trip (even if you are paid church staff). Use your vacation time like the other adults on the trip. This serves two purposes: 1) it sets an example of you being highly financially invested in the work, and 2) it deflates the pressure some will exert on you to meet their expectations for the trip. There will be people who believe if they are paying you…they own you. Some view the church with a spiritual-consumer mentality. They expect to get certain services, recognition, and power for their money. If you are not receiving anything but simply serving at your own expense and vacation time, you are freer to minister and you have greatly weakened the consumer's complaint when he is not happy with a real mission trip. Paul said in 2 Thessalonians 3:7–9: *"For you yourselves know how you ought to follow our example, because we did not act in an undisciplined manner among you, nor did we eat anyone's bread without paying for it, but with labor and hardship we kept working night and day so that we would not be a burden to any of you; not because we do not have the right to this, but in order to offer ourselves as a model for you, so that you would follow our example."*

the real gospel).[11] **The groups are also prepared - trained - equipped to engage in meeting the physical needs of the people they share the gospel with.**[12]

> **Deuteronomy 10:18:** *"He executes justice for the orphan and the widow, and shows His love for the alien by giving him food and clothing."*

You cannot substitute the true definition of preaching the gospel with social activism. Some try to claim that they "preach the gospel" by their works (a subject that will be addressed later in this book). The fake commission subtly dismisses the preaching of the real gospel and is content to engage in conduct the world calls *good.* **Like the Pharisees of old, the fake**

---

[11] We typically start with all mission team members completing a required daily Bible reading / study materials and prayer time that takes place for 50 days before the trip. We also have five required training meeting where we teach evangelism. A few days before we leave on the trip, the group puts its training to work by going out to engage in street evangelism. This gives them evangelism experience as well as sets a standard of reaching those in their own community before going somewhere else. A well-trained group results in an effective youth trip. Typically, our group of about 40 will reach an average of 1,500 people a day (including travel days) with New Testaments, tracts, skits and open-air preaching while on the trip. Group members will also engage in service projects which include painting, building, food and clothing distributions, etc.

[12] Each individual going on the mission trip has Christian service projects the person must do in his own community. Opportunities are available for several weeks prior to the trip. Some examples include ministry at a boarding school, serving at a vacation Bible school, yard work, painting, etc. All service projects have as their focus to share the gospel with those being helped. The pre-trip training in service makes an effective group when we reach our mission location. Needless to say, the Bible reading and service project requirements also serve as a good filter to prevent some youth from signing up for the trip. The unsaved church kid who is looking for a "cool trip" to get away from his parents may not be willing to commit to 50 days of Bible study and serving other people. Camp may sound like a better option to him.

commissioner is satisfied to engage in simply the externals of self-righteousness. The positive accolades from friends, service clubs, public charities, and religious organizations is comforting enough for him. Scripture warns us that such people are really "...*holding to a form of godliness, although they have denied its power; Avoid such men as these.*" (2 Timothy 3:5)

The truth is that communication of the real gospel, and good works are the two sides of a double-edged sword. The Great Commission will always have Spirit-led proclamation of the gospel, making of disciples, and the manifestation of *Spirit-led* good works. Titus 2:11–15 sets out what Biblical Christian service really is:

> "*For the grace of God has appeared, bringing salvation to all men, instructing us to deny ungodliness and worldly desires and to live sensibly, righteously and godly in the present age, looking for the blessed hope and the appearing of the glory of our great God and Savior, Christ Jesus, who gave Himself for us to redeem us from every lawless deed, and to purify for Himself a people for His own possession, zealous for good deeds. These things speak and exhort and reprove with all authority. Let no one disregard you.*" (Titus 2:11–15).

Note that our definition of missions starts out with a perspective of Holy Spirit-led love for God and others. Only this true love will cause us to warn people how to escape the judgment to come, and to truly care about their physical condition: "*One who is gracious to a poor man lends to the LORD,....*" (Proverbs 19:17). The Christian recognizes the brevity of his life and the severity of eternal damnation. Recognizing those two extremes makes clear that the first priority of care for another is to minister to the person's eternal soul. Some may say that they have seen people in such bad conditions that their physical needs must be taken care of and then sometime down the road preach to them (when they are ready to hear.) I have seen some terrible conditions too. The truth is that if you really want to, you can feed, nurse, build and rescue, while preaching the gospel. In about a minute or two you can share the gospel with anyone as long as he is breathing. Here is what needs to be remembered: One may look at the terrible ravages left after a natural disaster, or even the grotesque carnage of a body-scattered battle field and say it is "hell on earth." Maybe it is "hell on earth"...but *hell it is not.*

Unfortunately, many organizations and outreaches that call themselves missions are identified with a particular aid service or cause, and do not actively engage in preaching the gospel. To understand the first priority of preaching, ask yourself what need would there be for real missions if the day would come where the world had:

- clean water for *all;*
- healthy food for *all;*
- excellent housing for *all;*
- the finest health care for *all;*
- the best education for *all;*
- social justice for all
- no victims of human trafficking, and
- *every person* possessed a large bank account and retirement fund....

The answer remains the same. The need for true missions (the preaching of the gospel) would be just as great as it is today in our fallen world. Why? Even in a world free of physical needs, a person's ultimate need still remains the same: escaping the eternal judgment to come.

The ultimate enemy in a person's life is his sin and the second death. Ezekiel 18:4: *"The soul who sins will die."* The statistic has not changed... 10 out of 10 will die sometime during their life. Worse yet is the judgment that follows death: Hebrews 9:27: *"... it is appointed for men to die once and after this comes judgment...."* The gospel tells of the only cure for the ultimate enemy: 2 Timothy 1:10: *"...but now has been revealed by the appearing of our Savior Christ Jesus, who abolished death and brought life and immortality to light through the gospel."* The elimination of social ills does not save the soul. The most comfortable and happy life in the world has no value when the end is judgment to hell for one's sin. Jesus said as much:

> **Matthew 16:26:** *"For what will it profit a man if he gains the whole world and forfeits his soul? Or what will a man give in exchange for his soul?"*

This is not a book to theorize on the academic concepts of social justice and wealth distribution. I do not intend to belabor anemic terms like "balance" or "moderation" when discussing evangelism and good works. This is a fallible attempt at a "field book"[13] to comment on a couple of the many principles set out in the only perfect and infallible book, The Bible.

We are to warn others of the judgment so they too can know of the only way of escape from hell through salvation in Jesus Christ. This is why there is a Great Commission. The *Great Commission* is not defined by any person or by a religious organization. The definition and command to engage the Great Commission is made directly by Jesus Christ Himself:

> **Mark 16:15:** *"And He said to them, 'Go into all the world and preach the gospel to all creation.'"*

> **Matthew 28:18-20:** *"And Jesus came up and spoke to them, saying, 'All authority has been given to Me in heaven and on earth.* [19] *Go therefore and make disciples of all the nations, baptizing them in the name of the Father and the Son and the Holy Spirit,* [20] *teaching them to observe all that I commanded you;*

---

[13] A field book is defined as, "A book in which a surveyor or other technician …writes down measurements and other technical notes taken in the field." (Oxford Dictionary). I use the term "field book" in the sense that this book represents observations and experiences I have had in evangelism, missions and living the Christian life.

and lo, I am with you always, even to the end of the age .'"

What about those who say they "love Jesus" but disregard His commands? The reality is that they do not love Jesus. They are changing the meaning of the word love to some sentimental feeling. Jesus is the One who said in John 14:15: *"If you love Me, you will keep My Commandments."*

Do not be discouraged and quit reading! This subject of *The Great Commission vs. The Fake Commission* is very worthy of your time to study. A true believer does not want to end up seeing his lifework being burned up as hay and straw (1 Corinthians 3:12-15). We must remember, Christianity is all about Jesus Christ, not about us. The truth about what preaching the gospel means, must first and foremost be founded on Jesus Christ alone.

1 Corinthians 3:11–15: *"For no man can lay a foundation other than the one which is laid, which is Jesus Christ. Now if any man builds on the foundation with gold, silver, precious stones, wood, hay, straw, each man's work will become evident; for the day will show it because it is to be revealed with fire, and the fire itself will test the quality of each man's work. If any man's work which he has built on it remains, he will receive a reward. If any man's work is burned up, he will suffer loss; but he himself will be saved, yet so as through fire."*

You still have time to write the end of your life. Take for example the life of Alfred Bernhard Nobel who was born in Stockholm, Sweden, on October 21, 1833.[14] He was an engineer and a very successful chemist whose specialty was explosives and ammunition. He invented a detonator and blasting cap that would

---

[14] *Encyclopedia Britannica;* "Alfred Bernhard Nobel." *Encyclopedia Britannica Online 2014.*

mark the emergence of high-explosives. His invention made him a wealthy man. Later he invented dynamite. This too would be a huge success, resulting in great wealth and patents in both the United States and Great Britain.

In 1888 his brother Ludvig passed away while living in France. A French newspaper mistook Ludvig for Alfred and published a headline stating, "The merchant of death is dead." Alfred read his untimely obituary eight years before he would die. When Alfred passed away in 1896, his will left a large amount of his estate to create awards in chemistry, physiology, physics and literature. Yet he strangely also created one prize that did not fit the science/intellectual category... it was a peace prize—the famous Nobel Peace Prize. Many speculated that Alfred Nobel's founding of the Peace Prize was influenced in part to having read his premature obituary and pondered how his life work would be ultimately evaluated others.[15]

As Christians, we know that our work will ultimately be evaluated by God. Sit back and ponder how your premature obituary would read if it was written today. Will it simply mention your work, service club, help at a church and include the names of your family members? What about your obituary in light of fulfilling Christ's Great Commission? All of us know that there is so much more we could be doing to build the Kingdom of God and not my own kingdom. Yes, the thought leaves both you and me with our heads bowed and a little sick to our stomach. We are weak. We are sinners. We are not as faithful as we should be. In all that, we are also so thankful to God for His forgiveness in Jesus! The Lord in his mercy washes us, strengthens us, and sets us back on the narrow road. Jesus said, *"The things that are impossible with people are possible with God."* (Luke 18:27). Let us rise up to obeying the Lord's commands and changing that final obituary so we hear the words of our Master saying:

---

[15] The Nobel story and information is derived from *Encyclopedia Britannica;* "Alfred Bernhard Nobel." *Encyclopedia Britannica Online 2014.*

"...Well done, good and faithful slave. You were faithful with a few things, I will put you in charge of many things; enter into the joy of your master." (Matthew 25:21).

We live in a society where people are fascinated with rock stars, actors, athletes and religious/social activists promoting an endless number of causes. Despite the fact that some of these celebrities are living grossly immoral lifestyles, they are still glamorized for "how much they care."[16] This is a generation that is consumed with the *appearance* of caring, from colored ribbons, rubber bracelets, armbands, hashtags and other statements on social media. There is a subtle competition in making sure others know that, "I care more than you care!" As serious as some of the issues are, taking a public stand for the appearance of caring, is hypocritical and not the Christian standard.

The typical media-obsessed young person is naively impressed with the "photo ops" and scripted video of his favorite athlete or movie star engaging in great acts of kindness, or passionately advocating for the latest cause celebre.[17] The youth decides that he too wants to be viewed by others as a person who

---

[16] Like the hypocritical celebrity, staged attempts at righteousness have slipped into the church since its beginning (cf. *Ananias and Sapphira*—Acts 5:1-10).

[17] Scripture warns of a time when evil people and false teachers will disguise themselves as being righteous without God.
> 2 Timothy 3:1–5: *"But realize this, that in the last days difficult times will come. For men will be lovers of self, lovers of money, boastful, arrogant, revilers, disobedient to parents, ungrateful, unholy, unloving, irreconcilable, malicious gossips, without self-control, brutal, haters of good, treacherous, reckless, conceited, lovers of pleasure rather than lovers of God, holding to a form of godliness, although they have denied its power; Avoid such men as these."*

is "making a difference." Examine the following story to see how it plays out in your life.

Say you have a young person in your church youth group who attends a local high school. The student has a social studies teacher who is very popular with the other students. In class, the teacher openly espouses his liberal politics and impresses the student with his talks about caring for others, and disdain for "corporate greed." During the semester the teacher encourages his students to get involved in activities that he says will be "good for the community." He explains that such activities can include a wide variety of issues such as, "the environment, hunger, homelessness, racism, human trafficking, abortion rights, gay rights, bullying, or voter registration."

Here now lies the dilemma for your church youth-group member: Does the Christian youth: (a) hold a bake sale at the school to raise money to "save the world from global warming" or, (b) kindly engage in evangelism by visiting with some fellow students about Jesus Christ and then give them a gospel tract? The student knows in his heart how the two options will be viewed by his teacher and most of the students in the class. The bake sale will be smiled upon as a very small, but heroic attempt to not just sit by and do nothing as icebergs melt under the paws of stranded polar bear cubs! Some may even view him as an intellectual, because he is zealously advocating a politically-correct cause. In summary, his teacher will probably tell him that he is caring, and that he is "a role model for others who want to make a difference." Who knows...maybe the local newspaper or TV station will want to do a small story about him as a youth making a difference!

On the other hand, he knows that if he is passing out gospel tracts his actions are more likely to be frowned upon. His teacher may first gently correct him by telling him that there are, "many other ways to actually help people." If the student does not conform but continues engaging in witnessing, the response may get more direct. The teacher may point out (in front of other students) that he is, "not really helping people" but is "upsetting others when he shoves his religion on them." The teacher may also inject a veiled threat, that what he is doing is "against the law." Quickly the student realizes that he will not be receiving any compliments about how caring, giving, intelligent, open-minded or tolerant he is. Instead he is accused of being judgmental, narrow-minded, divisive, bigoted, and a bully who is engaging in "hate speech." The other so-called Christians in the class will get the message too...conform or suffer the same denouncement.

Stop for a moment and dig deep into your own life. How would you respond if you were that youth? Not many would continue forward doing what Jesus has told us to do—love people enough to tell them how to be saved. Many who claim to be Christian ignore true evangelism/discipleship and transfer off to some *ministry* other than their Biblically mandated main duty. Be honest with yourself. How do you want to be viewed? Many in the church are much more comfortable with dignified Christian service inside the walls of the church than to face persecution for the gospel in public. Maybe that dignified service is being a deacon, a Sunday school teacher, sitting on the mission committee, singing with the praise band, attending a Bible study, or even baking a pie for a fellowship. We all are given spiritual gifts to use for the edification of the church, but that does not nullify the work every Christian is called to do outside the church.

The average guy in a church men's group will be happy to get together to swing a hammer on a building project, but is unavailable to go door-to-door for an evangelism outing. A lady may be known and respected for her praying for "the lost" or "giving to missions," but she never actually evangelizes herself. As one said, "It is easier to talk to God about man than it is to talk to man about God."[18] Such a mindset will often be accommodated by some church leaders or pastors who recognize how little they

---

[18] Ray Comfort of Living Waters Ministry. His point is well taken. Obviously we are to do both, i.e. talk to God about man and talk to man about God.

actually share the gospel outside the church walls and their employment. Even though this is accepted as satisfactory conduct inside the church, it demonstrates a huge disconnect of claimed faith and the actions manifested from that faith. Jesus said:

> "For whoever is ashamed of Me and My words in this adulterous and sinful generation, the Son of Man will also be ashamed of him when He comes in the glory of His Father with the holy angels." Mark 8:38.

Let us move past the hypotheticals and take it down to you and me. If you were to identify yourself with the options of (A) or (B), below, which would you choose—be honest:

> A. You engage in social action (United Way, service clubs, food bank, sponsor an orphan). You also serve inside the church walls (either go to a Bible study, teach Sunday school, serve on a board, give financially, etc.). One time you went on a mission trip to "help people who were less fortunate." You have also gone to Christian conferences, seminars and even went on a "Christian cruise." You even try to "help grow the congregation" which means that twice a year you invite someone to church.
>
> > [The result of this choice is you will be viewed as a kind and helping person who is a solid and active church member. You will receive compliments and approving smiles by many both in and out of the visible church.]

Or

> B. You are faithful in the true church and in study of God's Word and prayer. You engage in real evangelism as a regular part of your life, out of love for God, and obedience to His Word. You have a true love for the unsaved, such that you tell them the truth about what God says

regarding their current spiritual condition and future destiny in hell (via word, tract, book, etc.). You also try to provide money, physical aid and do good works as scripture says you are called to. You go on mission trips that preach the gospel (with words and literature), and help with physical and spiritual needs while you are there. You are also willing to confront false teaching regarding the gospel. You know that you too are very weak and in constant need of God's mercy, grace, forgiveness and strength.

[The result of this choice is that you will be viewed as a radical. Some will say you are judgmental. You will not receive applause from those outside of the visible church, and very little within. Some in the church will say you are being a bad witness for Jesus because you are "turning people off by talking about hell." You will be instructed that you should witness by telling others, "how much God loves them just the way they are." A few friends will withdraw from you and some persecution will be felt.]

Most people in the visible church would rather be identified by others as "person A". Some may like to view themselves as "person B" but delusions aside, they choose a "person A" lifestyle. For those of you who choose to live as "person B" — despite the trials, tribulations, persecutions and false characterizations, you will be drawn closer to Christ. Your relationship with true brothers and sisters in Christ will become deeper and full of God's love. A joy that is indescribable will guard your heart and mind, even in bad times, because you are being true to Jesus' call and not the world's standards. 2 Chronicles 16:9: *"For the eyes of the Lord move to and fro throughout the earth that He may strongly support those whose heart is completely His...."*

The trials and persecution of the "person B" life should not take the disciple by surprise. He already understands that the unbeliever sees no value in Christ's death on the cross: 1 Corinthians 1:18: *"For the word of the cross is foolishness to those who are perishing, but to us who are being saved it is the power of God."* Jesus already warned us of the trials to come:

> John 15:18-19: *"If the world hates you, you know that it has hated Me before it hated you. If you were of the world, the world would love its own; but because you are not of the world, but I chose you out of the world, therefore the world hates you."*

This book is a call to end the fake commission. In part, it is a call to end going on short-term mission trips to poverty-torn areas with the sole purpose to repair something and not really share the true gospel of Christ. [19] Put an end to posting online photos of you "hanging out" with children to show "how much you care" (especially when you do not know their names). Put an end to saying that you, "are there just to love them" when you have no intention of sharing the gospel of Christ, and thus are content for them to end up in hell. End deceiving yourself that you are obedient to the Great Commission by attending endless Bible studies, men's groups, women's groups, youth groups, praise team practices, prayer meetings, board meetings, conferences, mission conventions, missional meetings and pot-luck dinners—if they do

---

[19] Short-term mission trips that are not focused on the Great Commission can become a great burden to the fulltime missionaries who are hosting the group. They feel saddled with the responsibility of providing a wonderful experience for those who arrive. Often this results in the missionaries abandoning their regular ministry duties to become quasi-tour guides and provide activities for the group. The problem is made worse if members on the short-term team are untrained and are simply looking for either an experience, adventure or something to put on their resume or college application.

not have as one of their major objectives to actually leave the church building to spread the gospel.

The true church is the God-ordained institution to equip the saints and send out missionaries. It is a beautiful institution! We as Christians are weak and frail, which is all the more reason we are completely dependent on the Holy Spirit to fulfill the work Christ calls us to—(part of that work includes evangelism.) The real Christian is not the one trying to earn his way to heaven. It is the ungodly who try to justify themselves through religious activities and periodically calling Jesus *Lord*. How devastating it will be for the false to hear Jesus say He never knew them:

> Matthew 7:21-23: *"Not everyone who says to Me, 'Lord, Lord,' will enter the kingdom of heaven; but he who does the will of My Father who is in heaven.* [22] *Many will say to Me on that day, 'Lord, Lord, did we not prophesy in Your name, and in Your name cast out demons, and in Your name perform many miracles?'* [23] *And then I will declare to them, 'I never knew you; DEPART FROM ME, YOU WHO PRACTICE LAWLESSNESS.'"*

Why do such a large number of those who claim to be Christians turn a blind eye to the *Great Commission* and embrace the *fake commission*? The answer can span the spectrum from being untrained, immature, fearful, disobedient, or at worst, a false-christian.

I challenge you to not feel hopeless; do not give up and quit reading! There is great hope for the untrained, the fearful, the immature, disobedient and even the false-christian. There is hope for even you and me! That hope is not in your talents, hard work, or determination, but in the power of God: *"Looking at them, Jesus said, 'With people it is impossible, but not with God; for all things are possible with God.'"* (Mark 10:27). Alright...you can keep going!

Questions to be addressed in the following chapters include:
- (Chapter 2)   What is the real gospel?
- (Chapter 3)   What is the Fake Commission?
- (Chapter 4)   What is true discipleship?
- (Chapter 5)   What about good works and the scripture: "*to the extent that you did not do it to one of the least of these....*"
- (Chapter 6)   What is the Great Commission?
- (Chapter 7) How do I get started effectively evangelizing?

To effectively address these questions, one must start with an examination of what is the *real gospel*. There are prominent Christian leaders who have voiced great concern that a significant sector of the visible church remains unconverted. One reason for this problem is that many have been presented with a false gospel, which results in false converts.

There is only one thing worse than being an unsaved person, heading to an eternal destiny of hell. That one thing is being an unsaved person, heading to an eternal destiny of hell — who thinks he is saved.[20]

---

[20] For a more specific clarification, when I make a general reference to the term "hell" I am referring to the final abode of the damned which is the Lake of Fire: "*And if anyone's name was not found written in the book of life, he was thrown into the lake of fire.*" (Revelation 20:15). When I make a general reference to the term "heaven" I am referencing the saved receiving eternal life: "*And the testimony is this, that God has given us eternal life, and this life is in His Son.*" (1 John 5:11). [Note that scripture teaches of a time where there will be a New Heaven and New Earth: "*Then I saw a new heaven and a new earth; for the first heaven and the first earth passed away, and there is no longer any sea.*" (Revelation 21:1).]

CHAPTER 2

What Is The Real Gospel?

"I solemnly charge you in the presence of God and of Christ Jesus, who is to judge the living and the dead, and by His appearing and His kingdom: preach the word; be ready in season and out of season; reprove, rebuke, exhort, with great patience and instruction. For the time will come when they will not endure sound doctrine; but wanting to have their ears tickled, they will accumulate for themselves teachers in accordance to their own desires, and will turn away their ears from the truth and will turn aside to myths." **(2 Timothy 4:1-4).**

The term gospel means *good news*. What is the good news? To understand the *good news*, you must understand the *bad news*. The bad news is that despite your positive and delightful thoughts about your own goodness, you have lived as an enemy of God,[21] a violator of His law, and one day will be rightfully judged by Christ to punishment in the fires of hell for

---

[21] James 4:4: *"You adulteresses, do you not know that friendship with the world is hostility toward God? Therefore whoever wishes to be a friend of the world makes himself an enemy of God."*

all eternity. [22] The *good news* is that by the power of God you can be forgiven and escape eternal punishment in hell. God tells you to turn from your sins and put your faith only in the sinless Lord Jesus Christ, as almighty God, who died on the Cross to take the eternal punishment for your sins, and believe in His resurrection from the dead.

If an accurate gospel is not presented, people will create their own, self-styled version of what it means to follow Jesus. One must realize that true Christianity:

- Is not about being rewarded with eternal life for being kind and helping the poor and weak.
- Is not about earning your way to heaven by living a clean life and doing more good than bad.
- Is not about getting to heaven by standing up each week at church and reciting the Apostles Creed or saying the Lord's prayer.
- Is not about earning salvation by engaging in a certain religious ritual such as: baptism, confirmation, penance communion, confession, prayer etc.

I use the term *visible church* to mean all that are in the church buildings and elsewhere who claim to be Christians. This *visible*

---

[22] Jesus said in John 7:7: *"The world cannot hate you, but it hates Me because I testify of it, that its deeds are evil."*

o   Romans 8:7: *"...because the mind set on the flesh is hostile toward God; for it does not subject itself to the law of God, for it is not even able to do so,"*

o   1 Peter 4:5: *"but they will give account to Him who is ready to judge the living and the dead."*

o   Matthew 13:49–50: *"So it will be at the end of the age; the angels will come forth and take out the wicked from among the righteous, and will throw them into the furnace of fire; in that place there will be weeping and gnashing of teeth."*

o   Revelation 20:15: *"And if anyone's name was not found written in the book of life, he was thrown into the lake of fire."*

o   Matthew 23:33: *"You serpents, you brood of vipers, how will you escape the sentence of hell?"*

church includes true Christians in addition to many unbelievers, false-believers and self-deceived.

I recall seeing the manifestation of the visible church first hand many years ago when I was with a well-known evangelist at a large Christian music festival. The evangelist engaged some attendees at the festival with individual interviews. All of those interviewed were asked if they were Christians. They all stated that they were. They were then asked to define what it meant to be a Christian. At this point the vast majority appeared somewhat stumped or confused. They would make generic statements such as "Jesus is my friend" or "I love to praise Him" or "He is always there to help me with my problems." The painful reality is that I do not recall one person who actually defined Christianity as the Bible does.

This problem of misunderstanding the gospel is not isolated to those outside the church doors. A large number who claim to be evangelicals may be doctrinally correct in one area of the gospel, yet distort it in other ways. For example, there are many who correctly claim that the Bible states that no one is saved by engaging in a religious ritual. Yet, these same people will cling to a religious ritual as the proof of their own salvation. What is that "evangelically approved religious ritual" used as proof a person is saved? *"The prayer."* A large number of those filling the church today believe they are saved from hell because at some point in their lives they repeated back a prayer that was given them to say, or to read out loud, or "follow along with." This is not simply in the church but this also occurs outside the church. If you do any street evangelism, you can find people who have no fellowship with other believers, no affiliation with a church, and do not read their Bible, but know that they are going to heaven because they "prayed to accept Jesus" at one time.[23] With that said, I think it is

---

[23] Obviously I am not saying that one proves he is saved by going to church, fellowshipping with Christians and reading his Bible and praying. Non-christians can do all of those activities and still not be saved. My point is that one who is converted will desire fellowship with the people of God and with God through His Word and prayer.

important to recognize that nowhere in scripture does it tell us that the *method* in which a person is saved is by reciting or repeating a prayer to *"ask Jesus into your heart."* Nowhere! Before you slam this book shut, tear your robe and yell "Blasphemy!"[24] I would encourage you to review what the Bible actually teaches. Do not bet your eternity on an evangelical tradition or methodology that has been popularized for the last 70 years.

Although some may be saved *while* saying a prayer (such as myself) it is not the ritual of prayer that saves. Conversion occurs only by the power of God. John 1:12–13: *"But as many as received Him, to them He gave the right to become children of God, even to those who believe in His name, who were born, not of blood nor of the will of the flesh nor of the will of man, but of God."* It is God who gives spiritual life to one who is spiritually dead—not magic words and phrases. The third chapter of John does not teach a person *how* to be born again but reveals that it is the power of God which causes one to be born again.

> John 3:5–8: *"Jesus answered, 'Truly, truly, I say to you, unless one is born of water and the Spirit he cannot enter into the kingdom of God. That which is born of the flesh is flesh, and that which is born of the Spirit is spirit. Do not be amazed that I said to you, You must be born again. The wind blows where it wishes and you hear the sound of it, but do not know where it comes from and where it is going; so is everyone who is born of the Spirit."*

One who is convicted by the Holy Spirit of sin, righteousness and judgment[25] and having been born again by the power of God,

---

[24] Matthew 26:65 (Caiaphas' phony conduct while charging Jesus with blasphemy.)

[25] John 16:7–8: *"... the Helper will not come to you; but if I go, I will send Him to you. And He, when He comes, will convict the world concerning sin and righteousness and judgment;...."*

will repent of sin and believe the gospel. He is not saved simply because he was willing to say a prayer sometime during his life.

You cannot find one example anywhere in scripture where Jesus or any of the Apostles teach people to *ask Jesus into their heart* to be saved. Scripture states in <u>Romans 10:9:</u> *"that if you confess with your mouth Jesus as Lord, and believe in your heart that God raised Him from the dead, you will be saved...."* The simple act to "ask Jesus into your heart" can be an act of man (Matthew 7:21-23). To truly *"believe in your heart"* unto salvation is always an act of God (John 3:3-8). The problem is that modern evangelism has substituted conversion by the power of God (John 3:3-8) with a manmade formula and ritual of insignificant decisionalism.

I have seen some people "say the prayer," and remain clueless on what they were doing. Maybe they agreed to say the prayer at a time when they were experiencing some difficulty in their life such as a financial problem or strained relationships. Maybe they were feeling a little guilty about something they had done. Maybe they said the prayer because their parents or a boyfriend or girlfriend wanted them to be a Christian. Still others may hear the part that God wants them to go to heaven and not hell—and they have no problem with that. They also hear that God wants to forgive and help them if they will just ask, "Jesus into their heart." Many will respond by inwardly saying, "Sure, why not, I will do what they tell me just in case this is for real." At this point the person will not become a Christian because he does not understand: 1) his sinful condition, 2) the judgment to come 3) his need to repent, 4) who Jesus Christ really is, and 5) why Jesus died on the cross and rose from the dead. The lack of spirit led knowledge regarding these five points make "the prayer" meaningless.

The evangelist who is quick to claim 232 people got saved last night at his rally because 232 people agreed to "pray" with him is misleading or is self-deceived. He has substituted the power of God with his power of persuasion. In summary, the outward act of "prayer" does not automatically result in regeneration and conversion.

False conversions often will manifest themselves later in the fake commission. This occurs because the false convert has a wrong view of Jesus. Christians frequently use terms and phrases they understand, but the unsaved person interprets them in an entirely different manner. I call these confusing terms and phrases *evangelicalisms*. Some *evangelicalisms* have truth in them but when conveyed to the unbeliever that truth can easily get lost.

For example, look at the following seven statements and see if you have heard variations of them used in evangelism. Perhaps they are terms you have used yourself when attempting to evangelize:

1) *You need to admit that you have done some wrong things called sin.*

2) *Your sin separates you from God and you will enter a Christless eternity.*

3) *Jesus loves you just the way you are.*

4) *Jesus died on the cross for you.*

5) *You can be saved by having a relationship with Jesus.*

6) *You will be saved and go to heaven by, "asking Jesus into your heart."*

7) *If you said "the prayer" never again question whether you were really saved at that moment.*

Let's breakdown these seven sayings and examine them:

> 1) *Admit that you have done some*
> *wrong things called sin.*

This is a statement that can be misunderstood by the unconverted. The non-christian may be willing to make a casual admission of sin without understanding the seriousness of sin. There is nothing honorable in simply admitting you are a sinner— it is simply the truth. Such a general acknowledgement of sin (or mistakes) is not the same as confession and repentance. I have found very few who at the time they, *"asked Jesus into their heart,"* actually believed, with *"godly sorrow"* that they had violated God's law and were justly damned to an eternity in hell. The Bible says in 2 Corinthians 7:10: *"For the sorrow that is according to the will of God produces a repentance without regret, leading to salvation, but the sorrow of the world produces death."*

R. C. Sproul writes, "When repentance is offered to God in a spirit of true contrition, He promises to forgive us and to restore us to fellowship with Him."[26] That promise is set forth in 1 John 1:9: *"If we confess our sins, He is faithful and righteous to forgive us our sins and to cleanse us from all unrighteousness."*

> 2) *Your sin separates you from God and*
> *you will enter a Christless eternity.*

I wince when I hear a weak-kneed Christian who cannot bring himself to use the word *hell*, but instead resorts to telling the unbeliever that, "Your sin separates you from God" or that he will "enter a Christless eternity." While it is true theologically that the unbeliever is separated from Christ (Ephesians 2:12), the phrase can be very misleading to the non-christian in his

---

[26] Sproul, R. C. (1996, c1992). *Essential Truths of the Christian Faith.* Wheaton, Ill.: Tyndale House.

darkened understanding (Ephesians 4:18). For example, many unbelievers think they are currently living *separated from God*...and frankly, they are comfortable with it that way. Some wicked think that after they die, the hell they are going to is a good-time honky-tonk where they hang out with all their buddies drinking whiskey and dancing with loose women. They will go on to say things like they would "rather be down there with their friends than stuck sitting on a cloud in heaven strumming a harp." This type of thinking shows how deceived they are about heaven and hell.

While it is true that the person in hell is separated from God's love, joy, forgiveness and salvation (e.g. 2 Thessalonians 1:6-12) it is not true that they are completely separated from God. The person who dies unsaved ends up squarely in the presence of God's judgment, wrath and hell (the lake of fire)...for all eternity.

> Revelation 14:9–11: *Then another angel, a third one, followed them, saying with a loud voice, "If anyone worships the beast and his image, and receives a mark on his forehead or on his hand,* [10] *he also will drink of the wine of the wrath of God, which is mixed in full strength in the cup of His anger; and he will be tormented with fire and brimstone in the presence of the holy angels and in the presence of the Lamb.* [11] *"And the smoke of their torment goes up forever and ever; they have no rest day and night, those who worship the beast and his image, and whoever receives the mark of his name."*

God made hell for Satan and his demonic angels. Jesus said in Matthew 25:41: *"...Depart from Me, accursed ones, into the eternal fire which has been prepared for the devil and his angels;...."* Satan is not the ruler of hell; God is. Satan ends up as a prisoner in God's hell. The unsaved are also eternally punished there.

The concept of Christ's redemptive work of reconciling a sinful man to a holy God is central to the gospel. Romans 5:10

states: *"For if while we were enemies we were reconciled to God through the death of His Son, much more, having been reconciled, we shall be saved by His life."* This concept must be explained to the non-christian. They must understand to be "separated from God" means spending eternity tormented in the Lake of Fire.

3) *Jesus loves you just the way you are!*

Without a more sufficient explanation, the nonbeliever may misunderstand this concept that, "God loves you just the way you are." Many non-christians take this phrase to mean that God does not really care if they continue to live a life of practicing sin, in full rebellion to God, because He already *loves them just the way they are.* This fatal misinterpretation marginalizes God to a grandfatherly figure, who knows you're a rascal, but responds with a wink and a smile while opening the doors of heaven to let you in...because He *loves you just the way you are.*

Yes, it is accurate to inform the unbeliever that while he is in his sin, God loved him so much as to make *available* forgiveness in Jesus Christ. Romans 5:8: *"But God demonstrates His own love toward us, in that while we were yet sinners, Christ died for us."* That verse needs to be read in its context. The next verse makes it clear that God's love does not result in Him winking at a person's sin, but rather that the penalty was paid through the death of Christ so that he can escape the *"wrath of God."* Romans 5:9: *"Much more then, having now been justified by His blood, we shall be saved from the wrath of God through Him."*

It is very important that the unconverted understands that his current spiritual status is not a buddy-buddy relationship with "the man upstairs."[27] He should be in great fear of God! *"It is a terrifying thing to fall into the hands of the living God."* (Hebrews

---

[27] "Man upstairs" is a term used by many of the unconverted as a casual reference to Almighty God.

10:31). The unsaved must realize that at this very moment, God's wrath rests upon him. John 3:36: "*He who believes in the Son has eternal life; but he who does not obey the Son will not see life, but the wrath of God abides on him.*" This means that the unsaved person is currently under a state of God's anger.[28] Psalm 145:20 says: "*The Lord keeps all who love Him, But all the wicked He will destroy.*"

There is a common cliché often spoken about those who unrepentantly practice sin. The cliché states that "God loves the sinner but hates the sin." This saying (which is not in the Bible) is often misunderstood by the nonbeliever to mean that God loves the unbelieving/unrepentant person so much that God neither sees him as a wicked sinner, nor will he judge him as such. R.C. Sproul demonstrates the folly of the cliché by pointing out that, "God does not send the *sin* to hell—he sends the *sinner!*" Psalm 5 obliterates the cliché when it tells us God's view of the unbelieving-wicked: "*…You hate all who do iniquity.*" (Psalm 5:5) In Psalm 5:6 the Word of God states "*…The Lord abhors the man of bloodshed and deceit.*" In Proverbs it states some specific conduct the Lord hates:

> *There are six things which the Lord hates, Yes, seven which are an abomination to Him: [17]Haughty eyes, a lying tongue, And hands that shed innocent blood, [18]A heart that devises wicked plans, Feet that run rapidly to evil, [19]A false witness who utters lies, And one who spreads strife among brothers.* (Proverbs 6:16–19).

One must understand that God is not spending his day gushing with sentimental warm and fuzzy emotionalism for the unrepentant/nonbeliever. God's thoughts are quite the opposite:

---

[28] *Merriam-Webster Collegiate Dictionary, 11th edn.* defines abide and wrath as follows:
  - o *Abide*: is defined in part as: To endure without yielding…. to remain stable or fixed in a state.
  - o *Wrath*: is defined as: *1.* strong vengeful anger or indignation; *2.* retributory punishment for an offense or a crime.

Psalm 7:11 NKJV "...*God is angry with the wicked every day.*"[29] Romans 5:10 explains that before conversion, the unbeliever is an enemy of God. "*For if while we were enemies we were reconciled to God through the death of His Son, much more, having been reconciled, we shall be saved by His life.*" This verse points out the power of God's love in that while we were His enemy, He provided a way for us to be saved through Jesus Christ's sacrifice on the cross. Why? Because He "*is patient toward you, not wishing for any to perish but for all to come to repentance.*" (2 Peter 3:9). God states in Ezekiel 33:11: "*As I live! declares the Lord* GOD, *I take no pleasure in the death of the wicked, but rather that the wicked turn from his way and live. Turn back, turn back from your evil ways!....*"

One should note that the very same chapter in the Bible that speaks of God's wrath (John 3:36) also contains the well-known verse about God's love, John 3:16: "*For God so loved the world, that He gave His only begotten Son, that whoever believes in Him should not perish, but have eternal life.* So which is it? Does God love the unbeliever or is He angry at him? The answer is both. If this paradox seems difficult to understand, ask your parents. They will tell you that there have been times they loved you but were also angry at your conduct/attitude and punished you for it!

God shows us His love by providing the way of escape from His judgment and wrath through His Son, Jesus Christ. This is explained in John 3:16-18. I must admit that I get very concerned when people quote John 3:16 but remove the context by neglecting verses 17 and 18. These two verses warn of the judgment to come. Look at John 3:16-18 and then you will see the perfect harmony it has with John 3:36.

John 3:16-18: "*For God so loved the world, that He gave His only begotten Son, that whoever believes in Him should not perish, but have eternal life.* [17] *For God did not send the Son into the world to judge the world,*

---

[29] The New King James Version. 1982 (Psalms 7:11).

but that the world should be saved through Him. [18] *He who believes in Him is not judged; he who does not believe has been judged already, because he has not believed in the name of the only begotten Son of God."*

It is a perversion to think that once you are saved, God leaves you, "just the way you are...." A true Christian cannot actively, willfully and unrepentantly *practice* sin because he is under grace and not the law. This false teaching is called antinomianism, which literally means "anti-lawism." The Word of God teaches the very opposite of antinomianism: Romans 6:15: *"... Shall we sin because we are not under law but under grace? May it never be!"* The Christian will struggle with sin and even at times fail, but he is not like the unregenerate who *practice* sin. The following five warnings must be made to the unrepentant who do not believe upon the Lord, but willingly *"practice"* sin:

(1) they are self-deceived,[30]
(2) they are slaves to sin,[31]
(3) they are not forgiven by God,[32]

---

[30] Titus 3:3: *"For we also once were foolish ourselves, disobedient, deceived, enslaved to various lusts and pleasures, spending our life in malice and envy, hateful, hating one another."*

   o   2 Timothy 3:13: *"But evil men and impostors will proceed from bad to worse, deceiving and being deceived."*

[31] John 8:34–35: *"Jesus answered them, 'Truly, truly, I say to you, everyone who commits sin is the slave of sin. The slave does not remain in the house forever; the son does remain forever.'"* (See also Titus 3:3 in the footnote above.)

[32] Hebrews 10:26–29: *"For if we go on sinning willfully after receiving the knowledge of the truth, there no longer remains a sacrifice for sins,* [27] *but a terrifying expectation of judgment and the fury of a fire which will consume the adversaries.* [28] *Anyone who has set aside the Law of Moses dies without mercy on the testimony of two or three witnesses.* [29] *How much severer punishment do you think he will deserve who has trampled under foot the Son of God, and has regarded as unclean the blood of the covenant by which he was sanctified, and has insulted the Spirit of grace?"*

(4) they are not Christians,[33]
(5) they are not going to heaven, but to hell.[34]

Some scriptures regarding the judgment of those who "*practice*" sin are set out below:

- Galatians 5:19–21: "*Now the deeds of the flesh are evident, which are: immorality, impurity, sensuality,* [20] *idolatry, sorcery, enmities, strife, jealousy, outbursts of anger, disputes, dissensions, factions,* [21] *envying, drunkenness, carousing, and things like these, of which I forewarn you, just as I have forewarned you, that those who <u>practice</u> such things will not inherit the kingdom of God.*"

- 1 John 3:4–10: "*[4]Everyone who practices sin also practices lawlessness; and sin is lawlessness. [5]You know that He appeared in order to take away sins; and in Him there is no sin. [6]No one who abides in Him sins; no one who sins has seen Him or knows Him. [7] Little children, make sure no one deceives you; the one who practices righteousness is righteous, just as He is righteous; [8] <u>the one who practices sin is of the devil;</u> for the devil has sinned from the beginning. The Son of God appeared for*

---

[33] 2 Corinthians 11:13–15: "*For such men are false apostles, deceitful workers, disguising themselves as apostles of Christ. No wonder, for even Satan disguises himself as an angel of light. Therefore it is not surprising if his servants also disguise themselves as servants of righteousness, whose end will be according to their deeds.*"

   ○ 2 Timothy 2:25-26: "*…with gentleness correcting those who are in opposition, if perhaps God may grant them repentance leading to the knowledge of the truth, [26] and they may come to their senses and escape from the snare of the devil, having been held captive by him to do his will .*"

[34] Revelation 21:8: "*But for the cowardly and unbelieving and abominable and murderers and immoral persons and sorcerers and idolaters and all liars, their part will be in the lake that burns with fire and brimstone, which is the second death.*"

this purpose, to destroy the works of the devil. [9] *No one who is born of God practices sin, because His seed abides in him; and he cannot sin, because he is born of God.* [10] *By this the children of God and the children of the devil are obvious: anyone who does not practice righteousness is not of God, nor the one who does not love his brother."*

- Matthew 7:23: *"And then I will declare to them, 'I never knew you; depart from Me, you who practice lawlessness.'"*

- Revelation 22:15: *"Outside are the dogs and the sorcerers and the immoral persons and the murderers and the idolaters, and everyone who loves and practices lying."*

Jesus said in John 14:15: *"If you love Me, you will keep My commandments.* One who is "born again" by the power of God, will have a true love for Jesus Christ, and faith in His Word, the Bible. The truly converted will turn from sin, will hate sin, and will no longer practice sin (1 John 3:4-10, Galatians 5:19-21, Matthew 7:23, Revelation 22:15). He is controlled by the Spirit of God and not the flesh (Galatians 4:6). It *does not mean he will never fail or sin* (1 John 1:8-9) but he will have a new nature and desires (Ephesians 2:1-10, Romans 6:17-18). The reality is that for your entire life, you will be constantly dependent and thankful for the unmoving grace of God and His forgiveness in Jesus Christ's sacrificial death on the cross.

4) *Jesus died on the cross for you.*

It is very important that the concept of Jesus' atonement is accurately explained to the non-christian. An unbeliever can take the phrase, "Jesus died on the cross for you" and dismiss it as a sentimental gesture or some general example of love.[35] Even

---

[35] Jesus did not die on the cross to serve as a political martyr or because He was overrun by an angry mob. Jesus had complete control over His

worse, an unbeliever can mistakenly think that *every person* is automatically forgiven and going to heaven because, "Jesus died on the cross for everyone!" This is the heresy of *universalism*. Jesus makes it clear that many people are not forgiven and end up in hell. In Matthew 23:15 Jesus speaks to a group of hypocritical scribes and Pharisees making it clear that they are *sons of hell*. In the gospels Jesus unambiguously states that *many* will not be saved.

> Luke 13:23–24: "*And someone said to Him, 'Lord, are there just a few who are being saved?' And He said to them, 'Strive to enter through the narrow door; for many, I tell you, will seek to enter and will not be able.'*"

In the book of Revelation, it plainly states that there are those who end up in the *"the lake that burns with fire and brimstone, which is the second death."*

> Revelation 21:6–8: "*Then He said to me, 'It is done. I am the Alpha and the Omega, the beginning and the end. I will give to the one who thirsts from the spring of the water of life without cost. He who overcomes will inherit these things, and I will be his God and he will be My son. But for the cowardly and unbelieving and abominable and murderers and immoral persons and sorcerers and idolaters and all liars, their part will be in the lake that burns with fire and brimstone, which is the second death.'*"

Jesus' atoning death on the cross is limitless in power and effectiveness. His atonement does not pay the death penalty and forgive those who die as unbelieving sinners. Jesus said in John

---

death and resurrection. John 10:17-18: *"For this reason the Father loves Me, because I lay down My life that I may take it again. [18] 'No one has taken it away from Me, but I lay it down on My own initiative. I have authority to lay it down, and I have authority to take it up again. This commandment I received from My Father.'"*

8:24: *"Therefore I said to you that you will die in your sins; for unless you believe that I am He, you will die in your sins."* Jesus said His death on the cross is the atonement for those who believe (His sheep):

> John 10:14-15: *"I am the good shepherd; and I know My own, and My own know Me,* [15] *even as the Father knows Me and I know the Father; and I lay down My life for the sheep."* [36]

The unbeliever must understand Christ's substitutionary death grants the Christian forgiveness because Jesus paid the death penalty for the believer's sins, and those sins are forgiven by God.

> "The death of Christ was substitutionary...in the sense that Christ is the Substitute who bears the punishment rightly due sinners; their guilt being imputed to Him in such a way that He representatively bore their punishment. There are many passages that emphasize Christ's substitutionary atonement in the place of mankind. Christ was a substitute in being made sin for others (2 Corinthians 5:21); He bore the sins of others in His body on the cross (1 Peter 2:24); He suffered once to bear the sins of others (Hebrews 9:28); He experienced horrible suffering, scourging, and death in place of sinners (Isaiah 53:4-6)." [37]

In summary: The innocent and perfect Lamb of God (Jesus) has taken the death penalty of guilty sinners (worthy of hell) who have saving faith in Him. This concept of Jesus' substitutionary

---

[36] Jesus says in John 17:9: *"I ask on their behalf; I do not ask on behalf of the world, but of those whom You have given Me; for they are Yours;"*

[37] Enns, P. P. (1997). *The Moody Handbook of Theology*, p.323 Chicago, Ill.: Moody Press.

death is essential to understanding the gospel. One either has received saving faith in the work of Christ on the cross to pay his sin-debt to God, or that person will be judged and pay for his own sins and perish (John 8:24, Revelation 20:12-15). That explanation is much more accurate and meaningful to the non-christian than the easily misunderstood statement of: "Jesus died for your sins."[38]

5) *You can be saved by having a relationship with Jesus.*

Often those who try to make the gospel message more appealing to unbelievers, will use the phrase "relationship with Jesus." The term *relationship* is an evangelicalism that means different things to different people. Think of all the various "relationships" you have in your life. You have different relationships with people through school, work, sports, hobbies, recreational events and even church. Some of those relationships are good, some are bad, some are important to you, and some are not. There are people whom you had a very close relationship with 10 years ago but now, they are not even in your life. Therein lies the problem of using the generic term "relationship" in reference to Jesus Christ.

Think of some of the celebrities and athletes who say they have a "relationship with God" or a "relationship with Jesus" but live habitually ungodly lives. Still others claim a relationship with a Jesus that is not recognizable from scripture. These folks come up with their own version of Jesus. Some want a relationship with Jesus where He helps them get out of their trouble. Others like having Him as a good luck charm to help them achieve success in sports or business. Many cults come up with their own type of relationship with Jesus that is devoid of the Jesus of the Bible.

---

[38] Obviously this was not meant to be a thorough explanation of the atonement.

Some evangelicals error by trying hard to create and market a Jesus that people will like. They want Jesus to appear "cool". Some want a Jesus who is a homeless social activist. Others want a Jesus as their magic genie who they can call upon to get their wishes met. Still others want a Jesus who is just as post-modern as they are—and would never judge anything as wrong. These evangelicals want to present a friendly Jesus who meets the people on their terms, conditions, and expectations.

Many of these evangelicals will then mistakenly tell people how much Jesus just wants to be their friend! This can create a false image in the mind of the unsaved of a little Jesus wringing His hands, hoping the person will like Him and invite Him into his life so they can have a *relationship*. The "relationship evangelist" does not dare turn off the person he is sharing with by telling him the truth. The "relationship evangelist" does not point out that Jesus is Lord and judge of all that have ever existed. He also neglects to mention that Jesus is the executor of the wrath of God, and that the unsaved will also be forced to bow and confess that He is Lord:

> Philippians 2:10–11: "*...so that at the name of Jesus every knee will bow, of those who are in heaven and on earth and under the earth, [11]and that every tongue will confess that Jesus Christ is Lord, to the glory of God the Father.*"

If we really care about them more than ourselves, we will tell them the truth about Jesus. Let us be careful to make sure people understand Jesus is Almighty God and we come to Him on His terms. Nowhere in scripture do we see Jesus pandering to His audience. Also recognize that Jesus warns the would-be disciple to count the cost before claiming to follow Him (Luke 14:25-33). Scripture also warns of the curse on those who preach a false gospel.

> Galatians 1:8: "But even if we, or an angel from heaven, should preach to you a gospel contrary to what we have preached to you, he is to be accursed!"

The *relationship* the Christian has with the holy Jesus Christ is that Christ alone is Master and Lord of all there ever has been, or ever will be. We, left to ourselves, are evil. The relationship that results is that of a loving Master and Lord who has redeemed from hell His eternally thankful children/slaves (Luke 17:10). As John Newton, author of the great hymn *Amazing Grace* stated late in his life: "My memory is nearly gone, but I remember two things: That I am a great sinner and that Christ is a great Savior."[39] We should all want our relationship with Jesus to be close, like family. Jesus tells us who His family is: Luke 8:21: *"But He answered and said to them, 'My mother and My brothers are these who hear the word of God and do it."*

6) *You will be saved and go to heaven by, "asking Jesus into your heart."*

The act of "asking Jesus into your heart" is not taught by Jesus or the apostles. The phrase is not mentioned anywhere in scripture. It is one of those evangelical*isms* which can be misunderstood by the unconverted. A friend once came to me concerned that his very young boy wanted nothing to do with, "asking Jesus into his heart." He said his son was very afraid to do so. I asked him what he was afraid of. He said his son was afraid to have someone living inside of his heart. It scared him! I suggested to the dad to drop the, "ask Jesus into your heart," language and actually talk to him about concepts such as his sin, punishment, hell, the Cross, forgiveness, heaven, etc. and what it

---

[39] Aitken, J. (2007). *John Newton: From Disgrace to Amazing Grace,* (p. 347). Wheaton, IL: Crossway Books.

means to believe in Jesus as Savior and Lord. He did that and the boy wanted to become a Christian.[40]

One who relies on the fact that some years ago he was talked into muttering some pre-made prayer about "asking Jesus into his heart," but never, by the power of God, repented of his sin and placed his faith in Christ's substitutionary death on the cross, has no Biblically based claim to conversion. John MacArthur describes it this way:

> "...the one who refuses to turn to God for forgiveness and salvation and therefore has no evidence, no good fruit, of genuine repentance. Salvation is not verified by a past act, but by present fruitfulness."[41]

7) If you said "the prayer" never question whether you were saved at that moment.

Really? How can you tell five seconds after someone repeats back a prayer (that you told him to say) he has truly saving faith in Jesus and is thus converted? Frankly, guarantying someone that he *truly repented, believed the gospel, and is forgiven,* immediately upon completion of a prayer appears to be a form of evangelical papalism.[42] I say this because I cannot know the person's heart. Maybe the person was saved, maybe not, only God knows at that point (Acts 15:8, 1 Corinthians 2:11). Scripture states that the examination of our faith is more than a statement of absolute assurance by someone who does not know our heart: 2 Corinthians 13:5: *"Test yourselves to see if you are in the faith;*

---

[40] That boy has grown up and, as a teenager, he has been on a couple of short term mission trips.

[41] MacArthur, J. F., Jr. (1985). Matthew. MacArthur New Testament Commentary (p. 70). Chicago: Moody Press.

[42] Sarcasm on the idea of a man bestowing salvation on someone.

examine yourselves!...." While scripture makes clear that those who truly believed are saved forever, I would be very slow to assure conversion to a person when only time will pan that out. 1 John 2:19 states: *"They went out from us, but they were not really of us; for if they had been of us, they would have remained with us; but they went out, in order that it might be shown that they all are not of us."*

Matthew 10:22 says in-part, "...*but it is the one who has endured to the end who will be saved.*" Theologically, this concept is called *the perseverance of the saints.* It means that the truly saved are manifested by their endurance of persecution over time. Note that Jesus spoke of this concept in the context of persecution. Persecution has a way of separating the *proud confessing churchman* from the true Christian who possesses eternal life.

Who are those who are saved? Jesus states that the ones who are saved are those who *persevere to the end.* This is not saying that the person who works hard to endure will earn salvation. Salvation and the ability to endure to the end are only from the grace of God and not something a person can generate. Jesus states plainly that our security is in Him, not our personal efforts:

> John 10:27-30: *"My sheep hear My voice, and I know them, and they follow Me; [28]and I give eternal life to them, and they shall never perish; and no one shall snatch them out of My hand. [29]My Father, who has given them to Me, is greater than all; and no one is able to snatch them out of the Father's hand. [30]I and the Father are one."*

How thankful we can be to God that it is He who keeps those who trust in Him from falling away. This truth is set out in Jude 24-25: *"Now to Him who is able to keep you from stumbling, and to make you stand in the presence of His glory blameless with great joy, [25]to the only God our Savior, through Jesus Christ our Lord, be glory, majesty, dominion and authority, before all time and now and forever. Amen."*

Now that we have cut through the traditions and evangelical clichés, we are ready to answer the question: What is the real gospel?

The Gospel

The gospel is not complex, but appears paradoxical. The paradox is that the gospel is simple enough to be understood by a young child, yet it is so deep that a great intellect cannot comprehend it. In resolving this paradox, one must understand that the knowledge of God comes only from God. Matthew 11:25 states that: "*At that time Jesus said, "I praise You, Father, Lord of heaven and earth, that You have hidden these things from the wise and intelligent and have revealed them to infants."*

God's plan is not for us to have a happy, carefree life, full of health and wealth. God's plan is that we *repent and believe the gospel.* For God "*... is patient toward you, not wishing for any to perish but for all to come to repentance.*" 2 Peter 3:9.

This is what the Apostles preached (and so should we!): Acts 20:21: "*...solemnly testifying to both Jews and Greeks of <u>repentance toward God and faith in our Lord Jesus Christ.</u>*"

This is what Jesus preached (and so should we!): Mark 1:14-15: "*... Jesus came into Galilee, <u>preaching the gospel of God,</u> ¹⁵and saying, 'The time is fulfilled, and the kingdom of God is at hand; <u>repent and believe in the gospel.</u>'*"

- To *REPENT* means to turn from your sins and forsake them by the power of God.
- To *BELIEVE THE GOSPEL* means that one who is "born again" by the Spirit of God (John 3:3-8) will:
  - Believe in Jesus Christ as Almighty God, who is without sin;
  - Believe in Jesus' sacrificial death on the cross as the only and complete payment for your sins;
  - Believe in Jesus' bodily resurrection from the dead on the third day;
  - Believe in Jesus as Lord over all things and confesses this fact to others.

[See the footnotes regarding the concept of "The power of God" and the scriptural support for the concepts listed above regarding what it means to "believe the gospel." [43, 44]]

It is that straightforward. Salvation has *nothing to do with* your self-righteousness, good works, engaging in a religious ceremony, or cleaning yourself up so that God will accept you. If you reject God's loving gift of forgiveness in Jesus Christ, you remain a guilty sinner waiting to be punished in eternal hell (John 3:36). If you *truly believe*, you are saved for all eternity!

1 John 5:13: *"These things I have written to you who believe in the name of the Son of God, in order that you may know that you have eternal life."*

---

[43] "The power of God" – when one is born again. Note that the concept of "believing in Jesus" is more than simply agreeing with some facts about Jesus. A person is spiritually dead and it is the act of God that allows one to see the kingdom of God: *"Truly, truly, I say to you, unless one is born again he cannot see the kingdom of God."* John chapter 3 is not an explanation on *how* to get born again; it is an explanation that it is a work of the Spirit of God. John 3:3–8: *"Jesus answered and said to him, 'Truly, truly, I say to you, unless one is born again he cannot see the kingdom of God.' Nicodemus said to Him, 'How can a man be born when he is old? He cannot enter a second time into his mother's womb and be born, can he?' Jesus answered, 'Truly, truly, I say to you, unless one is born of water and the Spirit he cannot enter into the kingdom of God. That which is born of the flesh is flesh, and that which is born of the Spirit is spirit. Do not be amazed that I said to you, 'You must be born again.' The wind blows where it wishes and you hear the sound of it, but do not know where it comes from and where it is going; so is everyone who is born of the Spirit.'"*

[44] For scriptural support of these concepts listed, see the appendix at the end of this book entitled: *A GENERAL OUTLINE OF FUNDAMENTAL DOCTRINES OF CHRISTIANITY.* (Note: Romans 10:9: *"that if you confess with your mouth Jesus as Lord, and believe in your heart that God raised Him from the dead, you will be saved...."* I use the plural *"Confesses:"* because the true believer's acknowledgement of Christ is not a one-time matter but an ongoing lifestyle.

R.C. Sproul wrote:

> "Faith includes believing in God. Yet that kind of faith is not particularly praiseworthy. James writes, 'You believe that there is one God. You do well. Even the demons believe—and tremble!' (James 2:19). Here sarcasm drips from James's pen. To believe in the existence of God merely qualifies us to be demons. *It is one thing to believe in God; it is another thing to believe God.* To believe God, to trust in Him for our very life, is the essence of the Christian faith."[45]

Despite all the evil you have done, God's Word says that a person can be forgiven and granted eternal life. The Bible says *in John 3:36: "He who believes in the Son has eternal life; but he who does not obey the Son will not see life, but the wrath of God abides on him."* Repent and believe the gospel TODAY, before it is too late! It is that simple and straightforward.

---

[45] Sproul, R. C., *Essential Truths of the Christian Faith*, Topic 64 – Faith (Wheaton, Illinois: Tyndale House Publishers, Inc.) 1992.

COMMISSION

CHAPTER 3

WHAT IS THE *FAKE* COMMISSION?

"For whoever is ashamed of Me and My words, the Son of Man will be ashamed of him when He comes in His glory, and the glory of the Father and of the holy angels." (Luke 9:26).

There are many who are content to raise their hands during worship, get out their notepad for the sermon, nod agreeably to the preaching and even say a prayer... but they are not willing to obey the commands of Christ. Why are we comfortable this way? The answer: This is the acceptable standard for the average attender in the typical modern church in the U.S. The need for evangelism/witnessing is proclaimed from *within* the walls of the church, but rarely executed Biblically *outside* the walls of the church. How do many congregations and individuals resolve this disconnect? The unbiblical, yet convenient answer is to apply the fake commission!

The fake commission accommodates a flexible man-made standard for evangelism and discipleship. The definition of the *fake commission* does not require the verbal preaching of the gospel. Many believe they have done all the evangelism they need to if they invite someone to church a couple of times a year. Easier yet, the fake commission allows one to change the definition of "preaching the gospel" to mean doing social work, yard work, or any other good work, even when you consciously do not use those opportunities as a springboard to tell people how to be saved through Jesus Christ.

When I speak of real evangelism, I mean the proclamation of the true gospel. God has chosen to proclaim His message through the, *"foolishness of preaching."* 1 Corinthians 1:21: *"For since in the wisdom of God the world through its wisdom did not come to know God, God was well-pleased through the foolishness of the message preached to save those who believe."* Preaching the gospel means that the message proclaimed is the Biblically accurate one.

Fake commissioners understand somewhere deep in their hearts that the real Biblical message is not well received. That is why cults, anti-christ's and religious charlatans will claim to be preaching the gospel when they tell people that God wants them rich and having, *"Your easiest life now!"*[46] Other false teachers will proclaim that their prophet, priest or religious leaders are the means to get you into heaven. Scripture makes clear that the true gospel will be an offense to the unbeliever. The offense is often manifested in ridicule and persecution aimed at the true Christian.

Herein is the distinction between the Christian who does not change God's message and the religious leader who attempts to market the gospel. The marketer will repackage the gospel to be more acceptable to the unsaved. This will result in a larger following, more contributions and little persecution. The false religious leader ignores the fact that the church is God's ordained institution and not the religious leader's personal organization. The marketer will determine that things are successful based on the large number of attendees. Worse yet, his worldly success convinces him that "God is on his side" and approves of his methodology and teaching. He will then place in positions of

---

[46] A purposeful play on the book "Your Best Life Now" by heretical teacher Joel Osteen. As one Christian leader said, "If this life on earth is your best life – that means you are planning on spending eternity in hell."

authority, people who are equally fleshly. Scripture is no longer the final arbiter of truth for him. With no accountability to scripture, so-called ministry and missions becomes whatever the religious leader wants it to be. To successfully market the so-called ministry and missions, he will use photos of helping the poor or act like he cares about people, and no one will ask any questions.

Why is the Fake Commission the predominant model for most of the visible church?

The first chapter mentions some of the reasons the fake commission is the predominant model for most of the visible church. The reasons span the landscape from true Christians who are untrained, to outright false-Christians. It should not go unnoticed that many who embrace the fake commission operate with a low view of the authority of scripture. They disregard scripture that does not match their lifestyle and ignore the hard sayings of Jesus. Their low view of scripture results in a self-style interpretation of scripture/prophesy: (2 Peter 1:20: *"But know this first of all, that no prophecy of Scripture is a matter of one's own interpretation."*)

People who deny the inspiration, inerrancy and authority of Scripture[47] may call themselves "Christian" but they are Christian in name only.[48] Jesus said in Luke 6:46: *"Why do you call Me, 'Lord, Lord,' and do not do what I say?"*

---

[47] Inspiration, Inerrancy and Authority of Scripture: Christ is the Word of God Incarnate: John 1:1,14; 2 Peter 1:20-21; 2 Timothy 3:16; Proverbs 30:5-6; Revelation 22:18-19.

[48] Matthew 7:21–23: *"Not everyone who says to Me, 'Lord, Lord,' will enter the kingdom of heaven, but he who does the will of My Father who is in heaven will enter. "Many will say to Me on that day, 'Lord, Lord, did we not prophesy in Your name, and in Your name cast out demons, and in Your name perform many miracles?' "And then I will declare to them, 'I never knew you; depart from Me, you who practice lawlessness.*

The dismissal of scripture's true authority will manifest itself in a life lived by the flesh and not the Spirit.[49] Those living by the flesh will be very sensitive to what the media, friends, coworkers, and the world think that Christianity *should* look like. This sensitivity to worldly views is in opposition with God's call. As James 4:4 says, "*You adulteresses, do you not know that friendship with the world is hostility toward God? Therefore whoever wishes to be a friend of the world makes himself an enemy of God.*" The world will make it clear to the Christian that he:

- Must not tell others how to live,
- Must not have a judgment or opinion that anything is sinful,
- Must not say the name of Jesus in public (unless as a curse word),
- Must advocate for politically correct objectives as proof that he is a good person.

Many in the church take the above cues into mind (consciously or subconsciously) when formulating their view of missions and personal evangelism. Recently I was visiting with a man who was looking at the possibility of starting a ministry which would engage in real-evangelism combined with an orphanage project. He told me that he had shared his vision with others who claimed to be Christians. Most of the responses he received showed great interest in the orphanage part, but somewhat cool indifference regarding the evangelism part. I call this mindset, "Mother Theresa syndrome." They want to view themselves as great caring and compassionate people who are giving to orphans, yet they are not as interested in doing what Jesus commands them first to do—accurately preach the gospel.

---

[49] Romans 8:5–8: "*For those who are according to the flesh set their minds on the things of the flesh, but those who are according to the Spirit, the things of the Spirit. For the mind set on the flesh is death, but the mind set on the Spirit is life and peace, because the mind set on the flesh is hostile toward God; for it does not subject itself to the law of God, for it is not even able to do so, and those who are in the flesh cannot please God.*"

The Christian's *first call* is not *simply* to help rescue and comfort one from a parentless existence on earth (as important as that is: James 1:27). Our first priority is to minister to the eternal need of all people. That need is to escape the judgment to come by being adopted into the Kingdom of God (Ephesians 1:5-14, Romans 8:14-17). Jesus spoke of His comfort and the Holy Spirit-presence given to His true children in John 14:18-21:

> *"I will not leave you as orphans; I will come to you. After a little while the world will no longer see Me, but you will see Me; because I live, you will live also. In that day you will know that I am in My Father, and you in Me, and I in you. He who has My commandments and keeps them is the one who loves Me; and he who loves Me will be loved by My Father, and I will love him and will disclose Myself to him."*

When you boil it down, the fake commission is embraced by many people, churches and para-church organizations for two fundamental and closely related reasons: 1) avoidance of persecution, and 2) the desire to be thought well of by others.

1) *Avoidance of Persecution:* Scripture tells us that the true message of Jesus is an offense to the unconverted (e.g. 1 Peter 2:8, Matthew 11:6, Matthew 13:57). The Apostle Paul explains that the unregenerate see no value in the things of God: 1 Corinthians 2:14: *"But a natural man does not accept the things of the Spirit of God, for they are foolishness to him; and he cannot understand them, because they are spiritually appraised."*

If you accurately explain to the unconverted his need to be forgiven, you will offend his sense of self-righteousness and religiosity. Everyone knows that if a person or a group claims that you offended them by something you said, you can face the whole gambit from censure to fascistic style retaliation.[50] Examples of this retaliation include: ridicule, slander, being mocked in class, excluded from parties, isolation and passed over for promotion (i.e. the American view of being persecuted). Let us not forget that we have brothers and sisters in Christ around the world who also face persecution for their faith in Christ. Their experience at times can be very different, but include: churches destroyed, homes confiscated, children taken, beatings, imprisonment, burned, beheaded or killed in other ways. BUT, if you engage in the fake commission, you can generally avoid all of these difficulties and still feel really good about yourself and your religious life.

2) _Desire to be thought well of by others:_ (i.e., man-pleasing). The second reason the fake commission is embraced by many is that we all desire to be liked, complimented and thought well of. This becomes a serious problem when it is more important to us than being approved by God: John 12:43: _"for they loved the approval of men rather than the approval of God."_ If you engage in social work and activism, you will be acknowledged and congratulated for your care and sacrifice. These people are honored by friends, religious organizations, businesses and even government agencies for the "good work" they do. You will enjoy the status as a person who is "making a difference" or "really cares."

In these social circles it is acceptable to have a Jesus who is either a social activist, homeless hippy or one who would not dare judge anything as wrong. It is not acceptable to have a Jesus who

---

[50] Webster defines _Fascism_ in part as: "...severe economic and social regimentation and forcible suppression of opposition ...." _Merriam-Webster Collegiate Dictionary, 11th edn._

warns of hell, calls people to repent of sin and put their faith in His sacrifice on the cross as the ONLY way to be forgiven. The Apostle Paul warns against the Devil creating an attractive deception in formulating a different gospel or Jesus: *"For if one comes and preaches another Jesus whom we have not preached, or you receive a different spirit which you have not received, or a different gospel which you have not accepted, you bear this beautifully."* (2 Corinthians 11:4). [51]

A true Christian, walking by the Spirit, has no desire to conduct himself in an unbiblical or offensive manner that brings shame to the gospel: 2 Corinthians 6:3: *"...giving no cause for in anything, so that the ministry will not be discredited,...."* Unfortunately some will attempt to use this verse to justify not telling others the gospel. They will explain that they choose to share their gospel in *subtle ways* so as not to offend people by "preaching at them." 2 Corinthians 6:3 does not excuse those who really do not want to preach the truth of God. The verses immediately following 2 Corinthians 6:3 make it clear that the faithful disciple who does not want to bring reproach upon Christ should still expect to suffer persecution, dishonor and slander:

> 2 Corinthians 6:3–10: *"...giving no cause for offense in anything, so that the ministry will not be discredited, but in everything commending ourselves as servants of God, in much endurance, in afflictions, in hardships, in distresses, in beatings, in imprisonments, in tumults, in labors, in sleeplessness, in hunger, in purity, in knowledge, in patience, in kindness, in the Holy Spirit, in genuine love, in the word of truth, in the power of God; by the weapons of*

---

[51] There are many verses on these subjects, but here is a small sample: Warns of hell: Jesus said in Matthew 5:22: *"...whoever says, 'You fool,' shall be guilty enough to go into the fiery hell."* Calls to repent: Jesus said in Luke 13:3: *"I tell you, no, but unless you repent, you will all likewise perish."* Calls to faith: John 11:25: *"Jesus said to her, "I am the resurrection and the life; he who believes in Me will live even if he dies,...."* Only way to be forgiven is in Jesus: John 14:6: *"Jesus said to him, "I am the way, and the truth, and the life; no one comes to the Father but through Me."*

righteousness for the right hand and the left, by glory and dishonor, by evil report and good report; regarded as deceivers and yet true; as unknown yet well-known, as dying yet behold, we live; as punished yet not put to death, as sorrowful yet always rejoicing, as poor yet making many rich, as having nothing yet possessing all things."

Paul also said in 2 Timothy 3:12: *"And indeed, all who desire to live godly in Christ Jesus will be persecuted."*

The Fake Commission Exposed

A true mission trip has as its first and foremost objective the *proclamation of the gospel.* Jesus said, *"...Let us go somewhere else to the towns nearby, so that I may preach there also; for that is what I came for."* (Mark 1:38). We see this on the missionary journey of Paul and Barnabas in Acts 13. They were prayed over by the church and then *"sent out by the Holy Spirit,..."* (Acts 13:4). What were they sent out to do? The next verse tells us: *"...they began to proclaim the word of God..."* (Acts 13:5).

Unfortunately this is not the case in the modern church where a short-term mission trip almost always focuses on some project of building repair/construction, soup kitchens, healthcare, human-trafficking, or other social need or issue. These projects may need to be done to further a local ministry, but they are not to be done as a substitution to proclaiming the gospel (which is often the case). Be honest and ask yourself if the mission trips you have been on had some special "project" as its major theme—or preaching the gospel as its major theme? These special projects, if there is time, should be done coinciding with the preaching of the gospel or as an addendum to preaching the gospel. Yes, Jesus healed the sick, fed people and showed compassion, but His focus was always to preach the Kingdom of God. Jesus said *"...Let us go somewhere else to the towns nearby, so that I may preach there also; for that is what I came for."* (Mark 1:38). When we show up on a mission, we should preach and say, like Jesus, *"for that is what I came for."*

I often get letters requesting financial support from those going on short-term mission trips. The typical letter explains how the group is *"going to show the love of Christ by_____"* (insert a social project). Unfortunately most of these letters say little or nothing about preaching the gospel. The ones that do, either call their social project "preaching the gospel" or mention evangelism as an afterthought to pander to those who think it should happen. One thing is clear, they are proud to appeal to me regarding their social project as the main reason I should give. We would do well to remember scripture tells us that God *showed His love* for people by paying the penalty for our sins on the Cross—not with a temporary social project. If we truly want to go somewhere and "show the love of God" to others, our mission must be anchored with the message that God said demonstrates His love:

> But <u>God demonstrates His own love toward us, in that while we were yet sinners, Christ died for us.</u> *Much more then, having now been justified by His blood, we shall be saved from the wrath of God through Him. For if while we were enemies we were reconciled to God through the death of His Son, much more, having been reconciled, we shall be saved by His life."* (Romans 5:8–10).

Some churches try to pacify their mission trip's lack of evangelism by tagging on a small non-threatening outreach…if they have time. For example, a group may spend 85% of its mission effort and money constructing a building and then combine a small kiddie program, or a small evangelism outing to dispense with the guilt that it is not really evangelism focused. Yes, God definitely wants us to reach children with the gospel and I have helped for a couple of decades with kids' evangelism programs and vacation Bible schools. Do not miss my point! Over many years, I have observed adults and young people who are happy to help with kids' programs to avoid the ridicule and persecution that may occur from public evangelism to their peers. If you doubt me, ask yourself how many adults show up with a smile on their faces to help with a vacation Bible school/children's ministry as compared to showing up with a smile to go engage in "door-to-door evangelism."

Recently I ran into a person who had been in Africa on a mission trip. I asked her what she did. She explained that the group tried to help some of the locals learn some business ideas[52] and employment skills in addition to other helps. I asked if they did any gospel evangelism. She sheepishly said, "No...but the people we helped knew we were with the church." So let me get this right: The person just spent thousands of mission dollars to share a few little business ideas, and we are left to hope (by osmosis) it will cause the recipients to run over to the church, fall on their knees and ask, "what must I do to be saved?" No, that will not happen. What if while spending all the time teaching the people how to obtain employable skills, at the end of each day, you gather the participants for five minutes and share the gospel and even send them home with a tract or a Bible?

A physician told me that many of the medical missions he is informed about, focus almost exclusively on medical matters with little or no objective to share the gospel. Opportunities are further squandered when no serious follow-up is conducted by the local church or sponsoring mission organization.

This type of reclassifying of the Great Commission, along with man-made definitions of missions, is all too common in the church today. Part of the problem is that the redefining goes unchecked by church leadership. For example, a youth group goes on a mission to a local assisted-living facility to play bingo with the elderly residents. Many of the residents are in the twilight of their lives and soon to enter eternity. It sounds like a great opportunity for outreach. The youth and their leaders have the residents' attention for over an hour during the game. What are the elderly residents told by the church during that time? Things like,

---

[52] I am an adjunct professor and have taught business classes at both the undergraduate and graduate level. Yes, teaching business principles can be a mission, but it is never the main mission, the gospel is.

O-61, N-45, B-10, etc....for an hour. Typically, not even a couple of minutes at the end of the game are spent telling them how to be saved from the judgment to come. If anything is said, it may be an advertisement about their church. But when it is over, the youth group members will feel good that they went and spent time with people and, "showed them how much we care." Such silence relegates the eternal power of the gospel message to the self-aggrandizement of a local service club. This result is the very definition of the fake commission.

Some churches will send their youth group to help at a soup kitchen and would not dare impose on the recipients by sharing the gospel. For example, several years ago I was asked by an organization to help put together a group from our church to supply a very large amount of food for a community meal for the poor. I decided that if we were helping supply the money, food and table service, we also would have our gospel tracts there and share the gospel. The social-religious person in charge did not want that to happen. Needless to say, I told her we appreciated the invitation but would decline. (I find many social-religious groups are happy to take the church's money and resources...but not its Jesus.) Interestingly enough, after we said no-thanks, the person in charge changed her mind and we ended up feeding the people, both body and soul.

Unfortunately most youth groups would have just gone along and missed the opportunity to preach the gospel and do a truly good work. The problem is that many youth pastors are content to simply announce in the church bulletin how the "youth served at the soup kitchen" (i.e. the fake commission.) These youth group leaders would do well to learn from the old soup kitchen missions that would feed the homeless and shamelessly have someone upfront preaching the gospel while they were eating (or require attendance at a short evangelism meeting immediately after the meal was served.)

Experience over time will teach you what the social gospel people already know: A crowd will show up for the stuff you are giving away, but very few will show up for the gospel. That is why social gospel people are thrilled with the large crowds at their events where they give/help/build, but never preach the true gospel. These large gatherings are also used as great photo opportunities for people back at the church, and for fundraising.

When our mission groups have clothing and food distributions, we have learned to preach first and then provide the physical needs. Why? Because when the free stuff is gone, the people will be gone. Most of the crowd is much more interested in getting their immediate physical desires met than seeking eternal life. Jesus pointed that out to the crowd of over 5,000 that He fed the day before:

> "Jesus answered them and said, 'Truly, truly, I say to you, you seek Me, not because you saw signs, but because you ate of the loaves and were filled. Do not work for the food which perishes, but for the food which endures to eternal life, which the Son of Man will give to you, for on Him the Father, God, has set His seal.'" (John 6:26–27).

The Apostle Paul's charge to the Christian is to preach the word as his true calling for evangelism:

> "I solemnly charge you in the presence of God and of Christ Jesus, who is to judge the living and the dead, and by His appearing and His kingdom: preach the word; be ready in season and out of season; reprove, rebuke, exhort, with great patience and instruction." (2 Timothy 4:1–2).

If we truly want to be faithful to the Great Commission, it is not hard to effectively share the gospel and engage in good works that glorify God—not the person. For example, say you are a dentist who is on a medical mission team and in comes a man in great pain. You can see that one side of his face is swollen. At the end of an exam you have determined that the source of the infection is a dead tooth. You work on the patient and by the time it is over, he is already feeling great relief and is thrilled. You then give him a bottle of antibiotics and explain the directions on taking them. Your patient is so happy and thankful! You then take a quick moment to bask in the good feeling you have from helping this guy who could never afford to get help and then...you send him out the door and call for the next patient to come in. Who gets the glory? You do. What if instead of enjoying the good feeling, you took an additional <u>60 seconds</u> and said:

> "Jose, I want to tell you something my friend. I know you feel much better...but you are much sicker than you think. [Now you have this patient's full attention.] You and I both have a disease that if left untreated will not simply take our lives, but our souls...the disease is sin. The result of your sin is punishment in hell forever. The only cure for it does not come in a bottle of pills. It comes only from the blood of Jesus Christ.
>
> Jose, you must understand that Jesus died on the cross to pay the penalty of sin, which is judgment in hell. For that penalty of hell to be removed means that you, by the power of God, turn away from your sins and believe in Jesus' forgiveness. Jesus willingly died on the cross to pay the penalty of sin. Because Jesus was without sin, He rose from the dead three days later. Jose, it is possible for you to be healed from the judgment of sin and hell forever!
>
> Jose, I do want to thank you for coming in today and I want to thank you for your time. Please take one of these New Testaments as my gift to you. Is there anything else I can do for you? Do you have any questions about what I told you?"

There it is! The fake commission, transformed into the Great Commission in 60 seconds. Why would anyone who says he believes in Jesus, disregard what the Lord commands? You may say you do not speak the same language as Jose. No problem, just use a translator or make sure you have with you some quality gospel tracts in his language. I have preached in churches and open-air in foreign countries with translators. I know one dentist who could not speak the language, so he had a recording of a person reading the Bible in the native language playing while he worked on the patient. Think about that situation. The patient is in the dental chair and cannot do anything but listen to the gospel, in his language, while his teeth are being worked on.

If we really want to tell others about Christ, one does not have to be very creative to take advantage of *every situation*. This is why I do not believe there is a great need for a discussion on balancing the issues of preaching the gospel and good works. When preaching the gospel and good works are simultaneously pursued, we are effective. The reality is most of us prefer to not simultaneously pursue them. Instead we default to using our skills only to build, repair, buy or give—not engage in the Great Commission. Let us change that and focus on the redemption of Christ and good works for His glory:

> Titus 2:13–14: "...*looking for the blessed hope and the appearing of the glory of our great God and Savior, Christ Jesus, who gave Himself for us to redeem us from every lawless deed, and to purify for Himself a people for His own possession, zealous for good deeds.*"

I find it interesting that many, who classify themselves as social-gospel people, also deny the inerrancy and complete authority of the Bible. Since they do not believe the Word of God, they often do not define terms the same way the Bible does.[53] For

---

[53] Much of the visible church has lost its sense of discernment. It is appalling that Sarah Young can sit down and write whatever nice-sounding things she wants to pretend that Jesus "told her" and it becomes a "Christian" best seller. When she writes what she claims that Jesus (in the first person) said, she is honored by religious book companies instead of denounced as an utter heretic. The new evangelicalism permits redefining

example, they will claim that they too, "preach the gospel." I will then ask them to define what it means to, "preach the gospel." Some respond in a solemn tone saying, "it is being like Jesus...it is helping people." If you continue to press them on what that means, often their attitude starts to bristle with offense that you would dare challenge them. Often I will then hear them respond by saying they choose to "love people" and not just "tell people they are going to hell!" Notice how they frame the issue. The statement insinuates that if you warn people of the judgment, you are unloving or simply enjoy harassing people.

---

theological terms based on how one *feels*. In a post-modern society, one can decide for himself whether his emotional needs are better met by Young's version of Jesus—and not the real Jesus of the Bible. One can claim he believes in inerrancy of scripture, and simultaneously claim that it is insufficient for his touchy/feely needs. Young says: "I knew that God communicated with me in the Bible, but I yearned for more." Like Young, the Devil also was not content with God, and yearned for more. Scripture states that: *"Every word of God is tested; He is a shield to those who take refuge in Him. Do not add to His words Or He will reprove you, and you will be proved a liar."* (Proverbs 30:5–6).

I heard a Christian radio DJ reading Young's dribble on the air as a "devotional." I called him and asked the DJ about what he was reading and he said, "It is based on the Bible." He is incorrect. Young, citing *references* to God's Word, does not elevate her words to that of Almighty God. Claiming that Jesus is speaking because she hijacks biblically sounding language and slaps on a Bible verse citation is no different than Joseph Smith claiming his prophesies were from God when he tried to sound like God by using King James English (other times he would simply plagiarize portions of scripture from the King James Bible).

Young is an example of the complete lack of discernment in the church and why it is perfectly fine to disregard the Great Commission and substitute it with the fake commission. It is all a function of a low view of Scripture, a high view of worldly approval, and a strong desire to "feel good." The Bible states in 2 Timothy 4:3–4: *For the time will come when they will not endure sound doctrine; but wanting to have their ears tickled, they will accumulate for themselves teachers in accordance to their own desires, ⁴and will turn away their ears from the truth and will turn aside to myths.* May God grant us repentance (2 Timothy 2:25).

Many social-gospel people want a Christianity that fits their worldview. Often it is a worldview that labels themselves as good. Their error is based on a lack of knowledge and application of scripture. Jesus did not focus on organizing soup kitchens throughout the cities of Israel, nor did He hold political rallies seeking social justice from the Caesar. The Bible says that Jesus preached the gospel with words: Mark 1:14–15: "... *Jesus came into Galilee, preaching the gospel of God, and saying, "The time is fulfilled, and the kingdom of God is at hand; repent and believe in the gospel."* It is curious that the word *repent* is often absent from the lips of social-gospel people.

The reason we start with evangelism while engaging in good works is the result of Jesus' own example and what He told his disciples.

> "*But He said to them, "I must preach the kingdom of God to the other cities also, for I was sent for this purpose."* (Luke 4:43).

> "*And He sent them out to proclaim the kingdom of God and to perform healing."* (Luke 9:2).

Fake commissioners will often defend a mission trip where the gospel is not preached by saying they just, "wanted people to see Jesus through our actions." Another phrase often heard is, "we went there just to love on the people." What does that mean? It is often used as code language for saying the group acted real nice, gave people some stuff, took photos of themselves working, and…. never really told anyone how to be saved.

I was with a small group in Africa at an orphanage during the summer of 2013. The group helped feed the kids, clothed them, bought new bed mattresses, helped kids with their school work, took them to the zoo and the beach, and…preached to them every night, prayed with them every day, provided copies of the Gospel of John, provided a large set of Bible-story videos and the equipment to watch them after we left. The group loved the kids and their leaders by ministering to their spiritual and physical needs. So let us dispense with this saying, "we went there just to *love on the people*" as the evangelical way to say that we went on a church trip and did not engage in the Great Commission. I cannot think of anything more unloving than to have knowledge of how to be delivered from the future judgment to hell, and not tell it. That is not "loving them" it is *hating them.* Let me provide you an example:

> Say that I am your neighbor and it is about 1:30 a.m., and I see your house on fire. I know that if I go over and pound on your door yelling and screaming I will disturb your family's sleep, and the entire neighborhood will think I am an obnoxious nut. To protect my image as a "good guy"— one who is not extreme, I just call the fire department. They arrive 15 minutes later. The firefighters break into the house and barely rescue you. Unfortunately, the firefighters were just a couple minutes too late to save your three children who are 7, 4 and 2 months old. The horror of their screams along with the death of your dear wife is more than you can bear.

What will you think of me when you find out that I was aware of the extreme danger that your family was in...15 minutes before help arrived... *and said nothing.* You will not care when I say that I "was really surprised that the fire spread so fast!" What will you think when I say with a shy grin, "I did not want to look like some *neighborhood wacko* yelling and screaming at 1:30 in the morning"? Your blood is now boiling. You are not entertaining thoughts of what a reasonable, compassionate and winsome person I am. Instead, you yell at me: "You self-centered jerk! While my family was screaming and burning to death,... all you could think about was yourself and how YOU would look in the neighborhood!"

The fake commission crowd claims it knows what is going to happen (i.e. the judgment of hell), but they will wait for the right time to warn the person. I learned this lesson the hard way a few decades ago during a winter in college. There was a fellow student who I hardly knew. He seemed like a happy-go-lucky type. A couple of times I engaged him in some little "Christian discussions" before class. He seemed somewhat interested but I did not actually share the gospel with him. I suppose I was "waiting for the right time." Later on I noticed that he had not been showing up for class. I inquired about him, and I was told that he was wearing his heavy winter coat and committed suicide by jumping off a bridge into the icy river below. Thirty-two years later, when visiting the college and crossing a bridge, his face was the first thing that came to mind.

The New Testament does not support, "preaching the gospel...without words!" The gospel is spoken. That is God's ordained method.

> 1 Corinthians 1:21: "...God was well-pleased through the foolishness of the message preached to save those who believe."

> Acts 8:35: "Then Philip opened his mouth, and beginning from this Scripture he preached Jesus to him."

> 2 Timothy 4:17: "....so that through me the proclamation might be fully accomplished, and that all the Gentiles might hear; ...."

Some social-gospel groups enjoy their status as activists who do not offend non-believer's sense of self-righteousness by preaching to them. If they begin to entertain any doubts as to whether they are truly engaging in the Great Commission, those doubts are dampened by the admiration they get from others. If challenged about their silence, I have heard some say (with a hushed tone) that: "We are to *preach the gospel at all times and when necessary, use words.*" In saying this, they believe they have an iron-clad defense against any challenge (i.e. because all

Christians agree that they have been called to a godly life and good works).

The phrase, *"Preach the gospel at all times; and when necessary use words,"* is a false, man-made concept that has *"the appearance of wisdom"* (Colossians 2:23). For it to be true, one must erase the last words of Jesus, *"...Go into all the world and preach the gospel to all creation."* (Mark 16:15). Jesus' definition of "preaching the gospel" is clearly verbal and is not mute. Liftin states: "Deeds in and of themselves are never said to 'preach' anything in the New Testament. Wherever something is said to be 'preached,' that something is always verbal content."[54]

When one uses the phrase, *"Preach the gospel at all times; and when necessary use words"* he attempts to infer that he is not simply a talker, but engages in the real gospel...(i.e. helping people.) Not only does the statement, *"Preach the gospel at all times; when necessary use words"* have no basis in scripture, it is almost always wrongfully attributed to Francis of Assisi. Biographer Mark Galli authored the book Francis of Assisi and His World and he points out that, "no biography written [about Francis] within the first 200 years of his death contains the saying. It's not likely that a pithy quote like this would have been missed by his earliest disciples."[55]

The reality is that it does not matter what Francis or anyone else says when it contradicts scripture. Scripture teaches that all Christians are to strive to live godly lives before unbelievers, but a godly life is to be lived out of love for Christ and not to escape the responsibility of telling others the truth of the gospel. Galli further points out that the "Good news can no more be communicated by deeds than can the nightly news." This *silent preaching* of the gospel is a denial of the scriptural mandate to preach with words!

---

[54] Litfin, Duane (2012) *Words vs Deeds* p.42 (Crossway Press).

[55] See *Speak the Gospel* by Mark Galli, *Christianity Today,* post 5/21/2009.

> Romans 10:13–15: *"...for 'Whoever will call on the name of the Lord will be saved.' How then will they call on Him in whom they have not believed? How will they believe in Him whom they have not heard? And how will they hear without a preacher? ¹⁵How will they preach unless they are sent? Just as it is written, 'How beautiful are the feet of those who bring good news of good things!'"*

One writer points out that in scripture, the gospel is spread through proclamation. You need to look up these verses and accept this fact: Matthew 4:23, 9:35, 11:5, 24:14, 26:13; Mark 1:14, 13:10, 14:9, 16:15; Luke 9:6, 20:1, 3:18, 8:1, 4:15, 43, 16:16; Acts 8:12, 25, 40, 10:36, 14:7, 21, 15:7, 16:10; Romans 1:15, 10:15, 15:20,16:25; 1 Corinthians 1:17, 9:14-18, 15:1; 2 Corinthians 2:12, 8:18, 10:16, 11:4; Galatians 1:8-9, 11; 2:2, 3:8, 4:13; Ephesians 6:19; Colossians 1:23; 1 Thessalonians 1:5; 2:2, 9, 13.

You can go to a poor area in the world, spend millions of dollars and rebuild it so it looks just like your upper-middle class neighborhood. When you are done, you will notice that the people remain at their core—fundamentally unchanged. They remain lost, and heading to hell....just like your neighborhood. [Sounds like you may have just found your first mission field!] If you want proof this does not change people from the inside, look at the governments that have spent trillions of dollars fighting poverty. Huge housing projects, job training, welfare, food stamps, heating assistance, the list goes on and on. Why has this not eliminated the real internal problems of people decades ago? Since governments, with their vast wealth and spending, have not fixed the problem, am I so deceived to think my insignificant amount of money is going to buy salvation for them? No, but Jesus bought true salvation for people, and we are to tell them about it. It is their only eternal hope.

The physical needs of the world are endless. Jesus said the poor will always be with you and you can do good for them whenever you wish (Mark 14:7). Only the true gospel can change a person's eternal destiny, independent of one's temporal physical circumstances.

How does our view of scripture impact what we call "missions?" Let me give you an example. In one church, I knew a respected Christian young man who had a strong desire to reach his community with the gospel. He developed and executed a well-planned door-to-door evangelism project. His vision was for each home visited to be: 1) reached with the gospel; 2) prayed for; 3) informed of a church to attend if they were looking for one; and, 4) to leave them with a plate of fresh baked chocolate-chip cookies. After announcing the plan during church services only about eight to ten people showed up to go door-to-door.[56] Other attempts he made resulted in about the same turnout. Those who went were blessed and even surprised on how well they were received. Some of the families visited were in crisis. Most families wanted to be prayed for by the strangers, and every family appreciated the appetizing cookies.

Sometime later, the same congregation was informed of a project to fill tens of thousands of food-bags to be sent to other countries to be distributed by religious and secular groups. The church paid the organization around $22,000 to bring the event to its building. Approximately 280 people showed up for that work.[57] Most people put in their couple of hours of assistance. When they were done some said that they were glad they came, and that, "it made them feel good inside."

Most of us like to have our so-called missions make us "feel good inside." You can build huge churches and other organizations if the people can leave saying that they, "feel good inside." Unfortunately, that is not the measure of successful ministry. Instead of making sure, "I feel blessed" we are to *bless the Lord,*

---

[56] 2011

[57] 2013

oh my soul." [58] We all battle the fleshly desires of self-approval as well as approval from others. Some mistakenly serve in the church believing that if they are approved by important people in the church, they are approved by God. Remember, it was the fleshly desire for approval from church leaders that resulted in judgment for *Ananias and Sapphira* (Acts 5:1-14).

All of our concerns for worldly approval will evaporate when we remember that we are to be more concerned with what God thinks of our service, than what others think. Paul understood this when he said: *"For am I now seeking the favor of men, or of God? Or am I striving to please men? If I were still trying to please men, I would not be a bond-servant of Christ.* (Galatians 1:10). Our service to God should not be sloppy or second rate. We should have a holy fear of God, not a fear of man: *"If you address as Father the One who impartially judges according to each one's work, conduct yourselves in fear during the time of your stay on earth;...."* (1 Peter 1:17).

True Christians are not ashamed of the gospel message. On the other hand, false believers will use service projects to camouflage their shame of the real gospel message—Jesus Christ. Paul understood the importance and power of the real gospel message:

> Romans 1:16-17: *"For I am not ashamed of the gospel, for it is the power of God for salvation to everyone who believes, to the Jew first and also to the Greek.* [17] *For in it the righteousness of God is revealed from faith to faith; as it is written, 'BUT THE RIGHTEOUS man SHALL LIVE BY FAITH.'"*

Jesus is the One who defines the Great Commission, not us, or the world around us. We do not get to re-write the objectives and methods. It is not the object of missions to make us feel good, but to accurately fulfill the call of our Lord. Mark 16:15: *"And He*

---

[58] (Psalm 103)

said to them, "Go into all the world and preach the gospel to all creation." There is not a "hole in the gospel," we just do not wholly obey it. The gospel does not set up a diametrically opposed view of either preaching salvation or meeting physical needs. The gospel demands the preaching of the good news along with a servant's heart of compassion.

The term *missions* has become very blurred. Corporations have a "mission statement." An individual may say that he is on a "personal mission." Some churches are quick to call anything that has the appearance of a good deed, *missions*, regardless of whether it is grounded in Biblical truth. Jesus states clearly that God desires those who worship Him, to do so in spirit and in truth: *"But an hour is coming, and now is, when the true worshipers will worship the Father in spirit and truth; for such people the Father seeks to be His worshipers."* (John 4:23). When evaluating a mission to engage in or support, you must look past the surface appearances and view it through the lens of God's word. This evaluation will include 1) a thorough review of the mission's doctrinal statement, 2) a review of the mission's *actual application* of the claimed doctrinal statement, 3) biblical accountability (financial, ethical and moral) and 4) whether the organization's fundamental commitment is to communicating the gospel to the unsaved. We must not blindly call a *Christian mission* anything that appears *good*. Take the example of the food bags mentioned earlier. Christian and non-Christian everywhere agree that feeding the hungry is a great thing. If we move past the superficial "feel good," did the church *really* accomplish Jesus' definition of the Great Commission—which clearly includes preaching *the gospel to all creation* (Mark 16:15), making disciples, baptizing disciples, and teaching them to obey all the commandments of Christ (Matthew 28:19-20).? Let's examine this project in four ways based on scriptural analysis:

1) You "partner" with an organization who states it is Christian. What does the organization think it means to be Christian? The closest statement it makes regarding Biblical Christianity is ("We believe there is one God, in three persons: Father, Son and the Holy Spirit. He

has directed us to help others in need.") Although this may sound good, it is far from a proof-text that it is Christian. A non-christian can believe this statement. Satan believes that statement (and will never be saved). Many cults (like Mormons) will say they believe in The Father, Son and Holy Spirit. If you study these cults, you find out that it is not the same Father, Son and Holy Spirit of the Bible. For example, the Mormon Jesus is an elder spirit brother to Satan. My point is that one should not automatically decide that a ministry is truly Biblically sound because of a general Trinitarian statement along with a claim to try to listen to Jesus and follow His will. Even cults can assert the same.

What else does the organization offer to support its Christianity? Nowhere does it claim adherence to other fundamental doctrines of the faith such as: inerrancy of God's Word; virgin birth; sinlessness of Christ; His miracles; His lordship; the fall of man/human depravity; judgment for sin resulting in eternal condemnation in hell; and salvation from hell only by God's grace through faith in Jesus Christ and His sacrificial payment for sin by His death on the cross and nothing else (to name a few). Right off the bat, you know there is a very serious problem when the fundamentals of the true Christian faith are ignored behind the banner of "Christian" and feeding people. Helping the poor and feeding the hungry is something all Christians should do, but feeding people does not make one a Christian.

2) The organization's employment application states it "celebrates diversity." This sounds positive, but then it makes clear it celebrates the "sexual orientation" of its employees. For an organization that claims to be Christian, this demonstrates a very low view/disregard for what the Bible says is sin. The Great Commission states that we are to teach others to obey all Jesus'

commands. How does the organization's celebrated position remain faithful to Matthew 28:20? Do you want your *Christian mission* led by an organization that advocates conduct in opposition to scripture?[59] Why not also have the church "celebrate" those who are unrepentant: liars, adulterers, thieves or child-molesting priests—or is it only politically correct sins that we will celebrate?

Christianity does not have certain sins that are bad and some that are acceptable. God's word says, *"Everyone who practices sin also practices lawlessness; and sin is lawlessness."* (1 John 3:4). Sin is sin, whether it is my sin or your sin. *We* are all guilty of sin and need forgiveness from Jesus Christ.

Christianity does not celebrate any sin, but it does celebrate God setting us free of the slavery of sin. In John 8:34–36: *"Jesus answered them, 'Truly, truly, I say to you, everyone who commits sin is the slave of sin.* [35] *The slave does not remain in the house forever; the son does remain forever.* [36] *So if the Son makes you free, you will be free indeed.'"* We see God's heart of forgiveness and restoration demonstrated in the response of the father in the story of the prodigal son: *"...'for this son of mine was dead and has come to life again; he was lost and has been found.' And they began to celebrate."* (Luke 15:24). Yes we are people who celebrate God's loving grace! In 1 Corinthians 6:9–11 we see summarized these

---

[59] The Old Testament law spoke against homosexual conduct (Leviticus 18:22, 20:13). The New Testament also speaks of homosexuality as a sin in both Romans 1:26-32 and 1 Corinthians 6:9-11. Those who claim that Jesus never spoke against homosexuality and homosexual marriage willingly ignore the Bible's clear teaching and the very words of Jesus in Matthew 19:4-6: *"...He who created them from the beginning made them male and female,* [5] *and said, 'For this cause a man shall leave his father and mother, and shall cleave to his wife; and the two shall become one flesh?'"*

concepts of the seriousness of all sin, the judgment to come, and forgiveness in Christ:

> *"Or do you not know that the unrighteous will not inherit the kingdom of God? Do not be deceived; neither fornicators, nor idolaters, nor adulterers, nor effeminate, nor homosexuals, nor thieves, nor the covetous, nor drunkards, nor revilers, nor swindlers, will inherit the kingdom of God. Such were some of you; but you were washed, but you were sanctified, but you were justified in the name of the Lord Jesus Christ and in the Spirit of our God."* **(1 Corinthians 6:9–11).**

3) The organization states that "We will encourage people of all beliefs to help us accomplish our mission."[60] It is God's design that the body of Christ proclaims the gospel and that all ministry foundation is built only on Christ: 1 Corinthians 3:11: *"For no man can lay a foundation other than the one which is laid, which is Jesus Christ."*

The Bible states that the truths of God are foolishness to the non-Christians: 1 Corinthians 2:14: *"But a natural man does not accept the things of the Spirit of God, for they are foolishness to him; and he cannot understand them, because they are spiritually appraised."* Some organizations can accomplish their *mission* with non-believers, but Christianity's true mission (of preaching the gospel) is accomplished by those filled and led by the Holy Spirit (i.e. those who have been saved by Christ).

---

[60] "Our Commitment to Excellence" statement. (Information per online publication on 8-2014).

4) Finally, the organization states clearly that when it distributes the food packs, the organization *does not* deliver a Christian message. Real Christianity delivers the eternal life-giving message of the gospel of Jesus Christ. If there is no real Jesus—there is no real Christianity! I will not support a so-called "Christian mission" that does not clearly proclaim sound Christian doctrine and worse yet, commits to the position that their specific organization *will not give the gospel message while doing its service.*[61] There are many outstanding Christian relief organizations who meet all kinds of needs of the poor, hungry and orphaned—along with sound doctrine and a clear presentation of the gospel! These groups are those whose Christian name should receive strong support from Christ's followers. The message of God matters most. As it states in Deuteronomy 8:3: *"...that He might make you understand that man does not live by bread alone, but man lives by everything that proceeds out of the mouth of the Lord."*

---

[61] They state in their FAQ:

> [Question] "Do you require delivery of a Christian message when the food is served?"
>
> [Answer:] "No. Our food is given to the neediest children, regardless of their faith or whether a Christian message is delivered...."

[Notice the straw man argument used: The question was not: "Do you feed only Christian children?" Yet their answer is skewed to infer that it was. The answer appears designed to shame the questioner by inferring that he is not interested in feeding hungry children who are not Christians. It is a statement that quickly diverts from the fact that it ignores the gospel message in its "Christian" work. Since the time of Christ, real Christians always shared the *life-giving gospel,* along with food, medical care, education, money etc., to all people regardless of their religion, nation, race, sex or orientation. Real Christians understand their own sinfulness and that nothing but Christ can heal them. Thus real Christianity will go to the ends of the earth to care and provide for more than just the body; it cares for the eternal soul that will live forever.]

Summary: So, after approximately 560 hours of work is done,[62] and $22,000 is spent for supplies, expenses and transporting the event to your church, what promise did you get from the organization in your goal to accomplish the Great Commission? None. So what? We feel good inside...we did a great "mission work" and the church received positive media coverage...we are missional!...Right?

Acts of compassion and care are a natural outflow of the gospel—*not a substitute for it*. Even young Christian children understand what a real mission trip is to accomplish. Recently, I was invited to speak to a group of young kids about missions. I started out by asking the group what they thought missionaries did. The answers came firing back with, "They tell people about God!" "They tell people about Jesus!" Not one mentioned any of the popular social causes in churches today.

If you have been a Christian for a long time you will notice there have been social issues that run a cycle in the church and society at large. During a particular cycle, some are more popular than others. At the time of this writing, a popular and important cause is "human trafficking" awareness. If you really want to be taken seriously in ministry, your church will take on human trafficking awareness as its *mission*.

Without question the buying, selling and abusing of others is horrific—it is Satanic. The problem is that some (not all) Christians speak passionately regarding their particular social issue...and it stops there! I end up hearing little about how the group is verbally preaching the gospel to those it is helping. Recently I received a support letter from an organization that has mentioned Christ in their trafficking mission. In the most recent letter I received, Jesus is not mentioned once. All people need transformation by God, not simply attempts at rehabilitation. Unfortunately some mission

---

[62] If you have 280 people, each working 2 hours each = 560 hours. Not including committee work, setup, media, etc.

groups are dimming the light on real evangelism while they brighten the light on their particular issue.

Some in the church are impressed by the image of being so daring and righteous to fight against human trafficking. Why is that same view not taken for evangelism? Why do some in the church fail to recognize that being released from "human trafficking" is a reflection of what the gospel is truly about! Jesus states that without the gospel a person is a *slave of sin*. Scripture makes it clear that the *slave to sin* is heading for an eternity in hell—a far worse existence then anything on earth. Being a slave to sin should be considered *spiritual* human trafficking. 1 John 3:8 states that "...*the one who practices sin is of the devil; for the devil has sinned from the beginning. The Son of God appeared for this purpose, to destroy the works of the devil.*" Why then are some youth enamored with fighting against human trafficking, but do not have an equal or greater passion for spreading the gospel? Many secular and governmental organizations are also fighting human trafficking. They are not preaching the gospel. Both the evil perpetrators of human trafficking and their victims need transformation by Jesus Christ's love. It is the preaching of the gospel of Jesus Christ that sets the captive truly free.

> John 8:34–36: "*Jesus answered them, 'Truly, truly, I say to you, everyone who commits sin is the slave of sin. The slave does not remain in the house forever; the son does remain forever. "So if the Son makes you free, you will be free indeed.'*"

[My personal note to those helping victims of human trafficking: Please understand my heart. I know it is a very important work. My point is the preaching of the gospel is the foremost call of the Christian, not simply social activism. I am sure there are many of you who agree with me. It is not preaching or compassion, *it is both*. For the record, I am not naïve regarding the seriousness of this issue, nor is it simply an issue of "awareness" to me. For more than two decades I have either prosecuted or via appellate advocacy, litigated to obtain or preserve convictions against kidnappers, rapists, child pornographers, child abusers, child rapists, a child manslaughter, and murderers. In addition, I have worked for many years regarding policy, legislation and other legal issues to protect society from convicted sex offenders. I understand the seriousness of this issue and appreciate your work.]

In summary: The true disciple's message is one of redemption preached and the manifestation of good works. I was reminded of this when, in another country, I was up on a mountain which provided a great view of the city. The local missionary with us said, "There are three things that last forever: God, the Word of God and the souls of men." That is why we engage in the Great Commission, because it is a person's soul that will live forever.

Titus 2:13–14: "...*looking for the blessed hope and the appearing of the glory of our great God and Savior, Christ Jesus, who gave Himself for us to redeem us from every lawless deed, and to purify for Himself a people for His own possession, zealous for good deeds.*"

CHAPTER 4

WHAT IS TRUE DISCIPLESHIP?

*"And He ordered us to preach to the people,
and solemnly to testify that this is the One
who has been appointed by God as Judge of
the living and the dead." (Acts 10:42).*

It is a false gospel that claims there is no cost in true *discipleship*. Being a disciple is not simply "donating" your time to help at church. It is not spending three minutes in the morning reading a "sentimental devotional." Jesus' call to discipleship is far from some evangelist's emotion-fueled plea for you to "ask Jesus into your heart."

Jesus makes it clear that being a disciple of His is neither temporary nor comfortable. He states in Luke 14:26-33:

"If anyone comes to Me, and does not hate his own father and mother and wife and children and brothers and sisters, yes, and even his own life, he cannot be My disciple. "Whoever does not carry his own cross and come after Me cannot be My disciple. For which one of you, when he wants to build a tower, does not first sit down and calculate the cost to see if he has enough to complete it? Otherwise, when he has laid a foundation and is not able to finish, all who observe

it begin to ridicule him, saying, 'This man began to build and was not able to finish.' "Or what king, when he sets out to meet another king in battle, will not first sit down and consider whether he is strong enough with ten thousand men to encounter the one coming against him with twenty thousand? "Or else, while the other is still far away, he sends a delegation and asks for terms of peace. "So then, none of you can be My disciple who does not give up all his own possessions."

You have probably heard very few (if any) messages preached on this section. I preached this section of Luke in Mexico some time ago. I started the sermon by asking the congregation how many of them were disciples of Christ? Enthusiastically almost all the hands went up. I then went on to preach (to myself and the congregation) for 45 minutes on these hard sayings of Jesus in Luke 14:26-33 and other sections of scripture. By the end of the sermon, I again asked the congregation, "So how many now want to be disciples of Christ?" A little less than half in the room raised their hands this time. Jesus' words in Luke 14:26-33 are not a recruiting speech, but rather a de-recruiting speech! How shocking it is to hear Jesus explain that our devotion to Him should be so absolute, that even love for family would appear to be hate in comparison to our love and devotion to our creator-God. *"If anyone comes to Me, and does not hate his own father and mother and wife and children and brothers and sisters, yes, and even his own life, he cannot be My disciple. (Luke 14:26).*

Jesus is very clear in stating that the price of discipleship is real, costly and decisional. It is real in that Jesus said, *"Whoever does not carry his own cross and come after Me cannot be My disciple...."* It is costly in that Jesus said, *"...none of you can be My disciple who does not give up all his own possessions."* It is decisional in that Jesus said, *"For which one of you, when he wants to build a tower, does not first sit down and calculate the cost to see if he has enough to complete it?"* One had better think this through very carefully before claiming to be His disciple, or *"asking Jesus into his heart"* as some refer to it. It is important to understand that nowhere in scripture does it say that a person can be saved by Jesus and simultaneously refuse to be His disciple. The words of Jesus in Luke 14:26-33 annihilate the popular view that if I say a prayer, Jesus will help me get the things I want during my life, and grant me fire insurance from hell when I die.

Luke 14:27 states: *"Whoever does not carry his own cross and come after Me cannot be My disciple."* In that verse, Jesus is not pointing specifically to the cross He would carry, but to the cross that His disciples would bear. In Matthew 16:24-28, Jesus addresses the subject of the cross by explaining that the true follower of His will have to, *"deny himself, and take up his cross, and follow Me."* The disciples knew exactly what Jesus meant (i.e. that they were called to die to themselves which included the possibility of physical death for their identification with Christ).

> "Only a few years before Jesus spoke those words, a zealot named Judas had gathered together a band of rebels to fight the Roman occupation forces. The insurrection was easily quelled, and in order to teach the Jews a lesson, the Roman general Varus ordered the crucifixion of over 2,000 Jews. Their crosses lined the roads *of* Galilee from one end to the other."[63]

Note that Jesus made a very similar statement about the cross earlier in Matthew 10:38: *"And he who does not take his cross and follow after Me is not worthy of Me."* Every person has a natural desire for self-preservation. But protecting yourself is not the view of the true disciple of Christ. One must be totally devoted to Jesus and hold nothing back, including the life *God has loaned you.* [64]

---

[63] MacArthur, J. F., Jr. (1985). *Matthew.* MacArthur New Testament Commentary (p. 199). Chicago: Moody Press.

[64] Notice that your soul was *loaned* to you by your Creator. The Lord says in Ezekiel 18:4: *"Behold, all souls are Mine;...."* Upon death, immediately a person's physical body returns to dust and his soul returns to God (i.e. all

A true disciple does not get bewildered and defect once the fires of persecution come his way. He has already been warned about them by Jesus, and assumes they are coming. Since he already views what he has as nothing, *"who does not give up all his own possessions,"* and his own life as already dead, *"carry his own cross...,"* he is better able to fight his own fleshly ambitions by the power of the Holy Spirit. He understands that persecution for the cause of Christ is an expected part of life. 2 Timothy 3:12 says, *"And indeed, all who desire to live godly in Christ Jesus will be persecuted."* Jesus Himself warned His disciples that they would be hated and killed because they were His followers.

> **John 15:18-19:** *"If the world hates you, you know that it has hated Me before it hated you. If you were of the world, the world would love its own; but because you are not of the world, but I chose you out of the world, therefore the world hates you."*

> **John 16:2-4:** *"They will make you outcasts from the synagogue, but an hour is coming for everyone who kills you to think that he is offering service to God.* [3] *And these things they will do, because they have not known the Father, or Me. [4]But these things I have spoken to you, that when their hour comes, you may remember that I told you of them. And these things I did not say to you at the beginning, because I was with you."*

During the summer of 2014 my wife, daughter and I were in Uganda ministering to some Christian kids at an orphanage. One day I asked the kids who wanted to learn how to evangelize. A group of about 10 headed out with us to some villages to pass out Gospels of John and a Bible bookmark that set out the gospel. This was the first time any of these kids had been a part of a

---

souls belong to God). Ecclesiastes 12:7: *"...then the dust will return to the earth as it was, and the spirit will return to God who gave it."*

public proclamation of the Gospel. It was exciting to watch as God opened doors for them to share with other Ugandans. The group was bold and effective. More importantly, the kids had *counted the cost* in their heart before we went.

While we were at one village a teenage girl from our group came to my wife and said, "see that man over there?" She then pointed to a man dressed as a Muslim. She went on to say, "when I gave him a gospel bookmark he told me that he wanted to cut my head off!" I was then brought into the conversation. I paused for a moment and told her not to let her heart be troubled. I paused again and then said "…what can I say—it comes with the territory." We both broke out in a smile and nodded at each other in agreement. She then headed back to the work. The rest of the group saw that she was unmoved by the threat and responded by quickly and joyfully returning to the work. She understood the cost of discipleship. She also understood the greatest need of the person who threatened her—as demonstrated by the letter I would later receive from her. [English is her second language so please overlook small mistakes]:

> "… Thank you…for teaching me about evangelism although some one told me that he will cut off my head when I was giving him a book mark and please you should pray for that person so that he can change and allow Christ as his savior…."

One who does not count the cost, but trusts in his own ability, well-meaning emotions and false theology will eventually result in folly and failure.

> Luke 14:28-30: "*For which one of you, when he wants to build a tower, does not first sit down and calculate the cost to see if he has enough to complete it? Otherwise, when he has laid a foundation and is not able to finish, all who observe it begin to ridicule him,*

saying, 'This man began to build and was not able to finish.'"

People can be *charmed* into church attendance, programs and even a false gospel. They cannot be *charmed* into salvation—it is a work of God.[65] Jesus said: *"...For this reason I have said to you, that no one can come to Me unless it has been granted him from the Father."* John 6:65. This is why we need to make it clear to the would-be disciple to count the cost. We should not consume ourselves with fleshly marketing techniques that make the church appear overly attractive from a "felt-needs" point of view. Those who have come along because they are impressed by the buildings and the crowds will not stick around if they hear the real message preached. Jesus points that out in John 6:63-66:

> *"It is the Spirit who gives life; the flesh profits nothing; the words that I have spoken to you are spirit and are life. "But there are some of you who do not believe." For Jesus knew from the beginning who they were who did not believe, and who it was that would betray Him. And He was saying, "For this reason I have said to you, that no one can come to Me unless it has been granted him from the Father." As a result of this many of His disciples withdrew and were not walking with Him anymore."*

The fake commissioner expects to be appreciated by others (not hated). He expects to be honored in religious circles (not thrown out). In summary, being ostracized, slandered, persecuted and killed is *not* what the *fake commission* disciple signed up for.

What should be the true disciple's response to persecution? It should never be self-pity or fear that God has abandoned him.

---

[65] Jesus said: *"...For this reason I have said to you, that no one can come to Me unless it has been granted him from the Father."* (John 6:65).

The disciple instead should rejoice that he is worthy to suffer for Jesus!

> **Acts 5:40-41:** *"And they took his advice; and after calling the apostles in, they flogged them and ordered them to speak no more in the name of Jesus, and then released them. [41] So they went on their way from the presence of the Council, rejoicing that they had been considered worthy to suffer shame for His name."*

> **Matthew 5:10-12:** *"Blessed are those who have been persecuted for the sake of righteousness, for theirs is the kingdom of heaven. [11] Blessed are you when men cast insults at you, and persecute you, and say all kinds of evil against you falsely, on account of Me. [12] Rejoice, and be glad, for your reward in heaven is great, for so they persecuted the prophets who were before you."*

How is a true disciple to respond to those who attack him? Jesus tells His disciples that they are to respond with love and prayer.

> **Romans 12:14:** *"Bless those who persecute you; bless and curse not."*

> **Matthew 5:43-45:** *"You have heard that it was said, 'You shall love your neighbor, and hate your enemy.' [44] But I say to you, love your enemies, and pray for those who persecute you [45] in order that you may be sons of your Father who is in heaven; for He causes His sun to rise on the evil and the good, and sends rain on the righteous and the unrighteous."*

I often wonder what the American church will look like when serious persecution comes (and it is coming!). How long will the large crowds continue to show up in the mega-church? What if the congregation's size starts to dwindle? What if there is a great fall off of the financial giving needed to service the debt on the beautiful church building? Will churches try to slow the defection by avoiding the teachings of Christ that could offend false converts or result in persecution? (Compromise with God's Word has already begun in many churches that were considered spiritually sound.) Maybe to keep the crowds, the church will emphasize more "felt needs" and become therapy centers to get help for your marriage, raising your kids, or watching your weight. Many U.S. mainline churches took that view decades ago. The consumer-driven church has always been a draw for many.

J. C. Ryle summarizes this section by showing that false disciples are nothing new:

> "Nothing, in fact, has done more harm to Christianity than the practice of filling the ranks of Christ's army with every volunteer who is willing to make a little profession, and to talk fluently of his 'experience.' It has been painfully forgotten that numbers alone do not make strength, and that there may be a great quantity of mere outward religion, while there is very little real grace. Let us remember this. Let us keep back nothing from young believers and inquirers after Christ: let us not enlist them on false pretenses. Let us tell them plainly that there is a crown of glory at the end, but let us tell them no less plainly that there is a daily cross on the way."[66]

Below is the entire article entitled: "NO RESERVES, NO RETREATS, NO REGRETS," of which portions were reprinted

---

[66] Ryle, J.C., *Matthew* (Expository Thoughts on the Gospels) (Crossways Classic Commentaries: v.1) p.59. Ryle (1816-1900) was known for his gospel tracts and preaching as an evangelical Anglican. He was the first Bishop of Liverpool.

from *Daily Bread*, December 31, 1988, and *The Yale Standard*, Fall 1970 edition.[67]

"NO RESERVES, NO RETREATS, NO REGRETS."

"In 1904 William Borden graduated from a Chicago high school. As heir to the Borden Dairy estate, he was already a millionaire. For his high school graduation present, his parents gave 16-year-old Borden a trip around the world. As the young man traveled through Asia, the Middle East, and Europe, he felt a growing burden for the world's hurting people. Finally, Bill Borden wrote home about his 'desire to be a missionary.'(1)

One friend expressed surprise that he was 'throwing himself away as a missionary.' In response, Bill wrote two words in the back of his Bible: *'No reserves.'* Even though young Borden was wealthy, he arrived on the campus of Yale University in 1905 trying to look like just one more freshman. Very quickly, however, Borden's classmates noticed something unusual about him and it wasn't his money. One of them wrote: 'He came to college far ahead, spiritually, of any of us. He had already given his heart in full surrender to Christ and had really done it. We who were his classmates learned to lean on him and find in him a strength that was solid as a rock, just because of this settled purpose and consecration.'(2)

During his college years, Bill Borden made one entry in his personal journal that defined what his classmates were seeing in him. That entry said simply: *'Say 'no' to self and 'yes' to Jesus every time.'*(3) Borden's first disappointment at Yale came

---

[67] I apologize that I cannot cite the specific author of the article but it does mention sources in the article's own footnotes.

when the university president spoke on the students' need of 'having a fixed purpose.' After hearing that speech, Borden wrote: *'He neglected to say what our purpose should be, and where we should get the ability to persevere and the strength to resist temptations.'*(4) Surveying the Yale faculty and much of the student body, Borden lamented what he saw as the end result of this empty philosophy: moral weakness and sin-ruined lives.

During his first semester at Yale, Borden started something that would transform campus life. One of his friends described how it happened: 'It was well on in the first term when Bill and I began to pray together in the morning before breakfast. I cannot say positively whose suggestion it was, but I feel sure it must have originated with Bill. We had been meeting only a short time when a third student joined us and soon after a fourth. The time was spent in prayer after a brief reading of Scripture. Bill's handling of Scripture was helpful...he would read to us from the Bible, show us something that God had promised and then proceed to claim the promise with assurance.'(5)

Borden's small morning prayer group gave birth to a movement that spread across the campus. By the end of his first year, 150 freshmen were meeting for weekly Bible study and prayer. By the time Bill Borden was a senior, one thousand of Yale's 1,300 students were meeting in such groups. Borden made it his habit to seek out the most "incorrigible" students and try to bring them to salvation. 'In his sophomore year we organized Bible study groups and divided up the class of 300 or more, each man interested taking a certain number, so that all might, if possible, be reached. The names were gone over one by one, and the question asked, 'Who will take this person?' When it came to someone thought to be a hard proposition, there would be an ominous pause. Nobody wanted the responsibility. Then Bill's voice would be heard, 'Put him down to me."(6)

Borden's outreach ministry was not confined to the Yale campus. He cared about widows and orphans and cripples. He rescued drunks from the streets of New Haven. To rehabilitate them, he founded the Yale Hope Mission. One of his friends wrote that he 'might often be found in the lower parts of the city at night, on the street, in a cheap lodging house or some restaurant to which he had taken a poor hungry fellow to feed him, seeking to lead men to Christ.'(7)

Borden's missionary call narrowed to the Muslim Kansu people in China. Once that goal was in sight, Borden never wavered. He also inspired his classmates to consider missionary service. One of them said: 'He certainly was one of the strongest characters I have ever known, and he put backbone into the rest of us at college. There was real iron in him, and I always felt he was of the stuff martyrs were made of, and heroic missionaries of more modern times.'(8)

Although he was a millionaire, Bill seemed to 'realize always that he must be about his Father's business, and not wasting time in the pursuit of amusement.'(9) Although Borden refused to join a fraternity, 'he did more with his classmates in his senior year than ever before.' He presided over the huge student missionary conference held at Yale and served as president of the honor society Phi Beta Kappa. Upon graduation from Yale, Borden turned down some high paying job offers. In his Bible, he wrote two more words: *'No retreats.'*

William Borden went on to graduate work at Princeton Seminary in New Jersey. When he finished his studies at Princeton, he sailed for China. Because he was hoping to work with Muslims, he stopped first in Egypt to study Arabic. While there, he contracted spinal meningitis. Within a month, 25-year-old William Borden was dead.

When news of William Whiting Borden's death was cabled back to the U.S., the story was carried by nearly every American newspaper. 'A wave of sorrow went round the world . . . Borden not only gave (away) his wealth, but himself, in a way so joyous and natural that it (seemed) a privilege rather than a sacrifice' wrote Mary Taylor in her introduction to his biography.(10) Was Borden's untimely death a waste? Not in God's plan. Prior to his death, Borden had written two more words in his Bible. Underneath the words *'No reserves'* and *'No retreats,'* he had written: *'No regrets.'''*

(1) Taylor, Mrs. Howard. Borden of Yale '09. Philadelphia: China Inland Mission, 1926, p. 75.
(2) Ibid., page 98.
(3) Ibid., page 122.
(4) Ibid., page 90.
(5) Ibid., page 97.
(6) Ibid., page 150.
(7) Ibid., page 148.
(8) Ibid., page 149.
(9) Ibid., page 149.
(10) Ibid., page ix.
Portions reprinted from Daily Bread, December 31, 1988, and The Yale Standard, Fall 1970 edition."

Disciple, remember…Jesus calls you "blessed."

> **Luke 6:22:** *"Blessed are you when men hate you, and ostracize you, and insult you, and scorn your name as evil, for the sake of the Son of Man."*

THE FAKE COMMISSION

CHAPTER 5

WHAT ABOUT GOOD WORKS AND THE SCRIPTURE: "...to the extent that you did not do it to one of the least of these...."

> "For by grace you have been saved through faith; and that not of yourselves, it is the gift of God; not as a result of works, so that no one may boast. (Ephesians 2:8–9).

The social-gospel crowd often will cite Matthew 25:45 in their fundraising material: "...to the extent that you did not do it to one of the least of these, you did not do it to Me." This verse is their proof-text to infer that feeding, clothing, healing, and visiting others, is what Jesus is *really* concerned about...not verbally preaching the gospel to people. Their promotional material can even carry a veiled implication that if you are not interested in supporting their social effort, you do not care about, *"the least of these."* The implication is often extended one more step to infer that you may not even care about helping Jesus (i.e. *"did not do it to Me"*). The most serious misinterpretation of Matthew 25:31-46 is that one obtains salvation because of the good *works* he does for, *"one of the least of these."*

A thorough examination of Matthew 25:31-46 *does not teach* that we should dispense with the preaching of the gospel because doing good works is the real way to earn salvation. Further, it *does not teach* that one is a "brother" of Jesus (i.e. part of the family of God) simply because he is poor, hungry, thirsty, sick, imprisoned or lacking adequate clothing.[68]

To understand this section of scripture, one must read it within its context and the timetable of the events told. The sheep and the goats are those who are alive immediately after the tribulation (v.31-32). The sheep are true followers of Jesus who are providing love and comfort to fellow Christians (Jesus' brothers) during the terrible tribulation time. The reality of their faith and love for Christ is manifest in their care and love for fellow believers (Jesus' brothers—even the least of them). Jesus said in John 13:34-35:

> "A new commandment I give to you, that you love one another, even as I have loved you, that you also love one another. By this all men will know that you are My disciples, if you have love for one another."

The goats are the hypocrites. Hypocrites (especially religious hypocrites) always view themselves in a light more positive than reality. The goats call Jesus *Lord* (Matthew 25:44) and claim they would have done the right thing if they were given the chance (v. 44). The reality is that they have no love for Christ or His followers. The goats are the *"accursed ones"* (v.41), condemned to *"eternal punishment"* (v. 46), and sentenced to the *"eternal fire which has been prepared for the devil and his angels"* (v. 41).

Let us examine this section of scripture in more detail:

> MATTHEW 25:31-46: *"But when the Son of Man comes in His glory, and all the angels with Him, then He will sit on His glorious throne. 32 And all the*

---

[68] Litfin, Duane (2012) *Words vs Deeds* p.192- 193 (Crossway Press).

nations will be gathered before Him; and He will separate them from one another, as the shepherd separates the sheep from the goats; [33] *and He will put the sheep on His right, and the goats on the left.* [34] *Then the King will say to those on His right, 'Come, you who are blessed of My Father, inherit the kingdom prepared for you from the foundation of the world.* [35] *For I was hungry, and you gave Me something to eat; I was thirsty, and you gave Me drink; I was a stranger, and you invited Me in;* [3] [6]*naked, and you clothed Me; I was sick, and you visited Me; I was in prison, and you came to Me.'* [37]*Then the righteous will answer Him, saying, 'Lord, when did we see You hungry, and feed You, or thirsty, and give You drink?* [38]*And when did we see You a stranger, and invite You in, or naked, and clothe You?* [39]*And when did we see You sick, or in prison, and come to You?'* [40]*And the King will answer and say to them, 'Truly I say to you, to the extent that you did it to one of these brothers of Mine, even the least of them, you did it to Me.'* [41]*Then He will also say to those on His left, 'Depart from Me, accursed ones, into the eternal fire which has been prepared for the devil and his angels;* [42] *for I was hungry, and you gave Me nothing to eat; I was thirsty, and you gave Me nothing to drink;* [43] *I was a stranger, and you did not invite Me in; naked, and you did not clothe Me; sick, and in prison, and you did not visit Me.'* [44]*Then they themselves also will answer, saying, 'Lord, when did we see You hungry, or thirsty, or a stranger, or naked, or sick, or in prison, and did not take care of You?'* [45]*Then He will answer them, saying, 'Truly I say to you, to the extent that you did not do it to one of the least of these, you did not do it to Me.'* [46]*And these will go away into eternal punishment, but the righteous into eternal life."*

This portion of scripture is the conclusion of what is known as the Olivet Discourse. This judgment by Christ is not to be confused with the Great White Throne Judgment[69] mentioned in Revelation 20:11-15. Likewise, it should not be confused with the Judgment Seat of Christ, where the believers are judged and rewarded for their work in the Lord (1 Corinthians 3:12-15).

The judgment in Matthew 25:31-46 is of those who are alive on earth at the time of Jesus' Second Coming *"...immediately after the tribulation...."* (Matthew 24:29). It is composed of believers and non-believers who survived the Great Tribulation.[70] The Great Tribulation survivors are either Christians or non-Christians (i.e. sheep or goats—Matthew 25:32). The judgment occurs after the tribulation and immediately before Jesus' millennium reign on earth.

It should further be noted that the two parables immediately prior to the judgment in Matthew 25:31-46 are the parable of the 10 virgins and the parable of the talents (Matthew 25:1-30). Both parables emphasize the distinction between the visible church and the invisible church. The *visible church* meaning all church

---

[69] The Great White Throne Judgment can also be referred to as the Judgment of the Damned. These are all non-Christians who are raised at the end of the 1000-year reign of Christ after the Tribulation. We will see in the verses below that these individuals will be judged to hell before the Great White Throne of Judgment.

> Revelation 20:4-5: *"And I saw thrones, and they sat upon them, and judgment was given to them. And I saw the souls of those who had been beheaded because of the testimony of Jesus and because of the word of God, and those who had not worshiped the beast or his image, and had not received the mark upon their forehead and upon their hand; and they came to life and reigned with Christ for a thousand years. 5 The rest of the dead did not come to life until the thousand years were completed. This is the first resurrection."*

[70] It must be recognized that there are Christians who are preeminent theologians, and hold different views on the subject of eschatology (end-times and chronology of the end-times).

buildings/denominations and all who claim to be Christians. This group includes many unbelievers, false-believers and self-deceived, in addition to true Christians. The *invisible church* (i.e. the *real* church) is comprised solely of those who are truly converted (the redeemed). These are the true Christians who do not simply perform lip-service to Christ, but are loyal servants going about doing their Lord's business.

The judgment in Matthew 25:31-46, of the sheep and the goats demonstrates there are plenty of goats who will call Jesus *"Lord"* (v.44), yet are not true Christians. Examine the judgment of the goats. They try to justify themselves by saying they too *would have* provided food/drink, shelter, clothes, to Jesus, if given the opportunity. If they had the chance they would have visited Him when He was sick or in prison! These *goats* are like the false believers we read about in the parable of the 10 virgins and the parable of the talents (Matthew 25:1-30). The false believers give deceptive (even self-deceived) appearances that they are real servants of God, except for the fact that they did not produce any Spirit-led good works.

> 2 Timothy 3:13: *"But evil men and impostors will proceed from bad to worse, deceiving and being deceived."*

> 2 Timothy 3:5: *"...holding to a form of godliness, although they have denied its power; Avoid such men as these."*

> 2 Corinthians 11:13–15: *"For such men are false apostles, deceitful workers, disguising themselves as apostles of Christ. No wonder, for even Satan disguises himself as an angel of light. Therefore it is not surprising if his servants also disguise themselves as servants of righteousness, whose end will be according to their deeds."*

The sheep (Christians)[71] do not earn their position from their good deeds, but by the grace of God. The sheep's good works are a mere manifestation of truly being Christians. Ephesians 2:8-10 sums both concepts up as follows:

> Ephesians 2:8–10: *"For by grace you have been saved through faith; and that not of yourselves, it is the gift of God; not as a result of works, so that no one may boast. For we are His workmanship, created in Christ Jesus for good works, which God prepared beforehand so that we would walk in them."*

The believer goes about doing good by the Spirit of God. Notice that the sheep (Christians) have not been keeping track of how much good they have done. These believers are hardly aware of their good works.

> Matthew 25:37-40: *[37]Then the righteous will answer Him, saying, 'Lord, when did we see You hungry, and feed You, or thirsty, and give You drink? [38]And when did we see You a stranger, and invite You in, or naked, and clothe You? [39]And when did we see You sick, or in prison, and come to You?' [40]And the King will answer and say to them, 'Truly I say to you, to the extent that you did it to one of these* brothers of Mine, even the least of them, you did it to Me.'

The true believer's (i.e. sheep) response is not an act of false humility, but simply the manifestation of being led by the Spirit.

---

[71] Jesus calls His disciples *sheep* in other passages of scripture. John 10:26-28: *"But you do not believe, because you are not of My sheep. [27] My sheep hear My voice, and I know them, and they follow Me; [28] and I give eternal life to them, and they shall never perish; and no one shall snatch them out of My hand."* Jesus is the "Good Shepherd." John 10:14-16: *"I am the good shepherd; and I know My own, and My own know Me, [15] even as the Father knows Me and I know the Father; and I lay down My life for the sheep. [16] And I have other sheep, which are not of this fold; I must bring them also, and they shall hear My voice; and they shall become one flock with one shepherd."*

In verse 40 Jesus says, *"to the extent that you did it to one of these brothers of Mine, even the least of them, you did it to Me."* In Matthew 25:40 the *"brothers"* are fellow Christians. These brothers are both Jews and Gentiles who have put their faith in Christ and endured the Tribulation.[72] This point is crucial in viewing the "least of these."

Recall that in Matthew 25:45, Jesus is speaking to the goats (the unsaved/damned) when they are condemned for their lack of mercy toward "the least of these." Who are the people that Jesus is referring to that he calls "the least of these?" The definition of the "least of these" is set out five verses before, when Jesus addresses the sheep (i.e. Christians) in verse 40: "And the King will answer and say to them, 'Truly I say to you, to the extent that you did it to one of these brothers of Mine, even the least of them, you did it to Me.' The "least of these" are Jesus' brothers (i.e. true Christians). Jesus said that his real brothers, sisters and mother are those who do the will of God:

> Matthew 12:48-50: "But He answered *the one who was telling Him and said, 'Who is My mother and who are My brothers?' 49And stretching out His hand toward His disciples, He said, 'Behold, My mother and My brothers! 50For whoever does the will of My Father who is in heaven, he is My brother and sister and mother.'"*

---

[72] Warren Wiersbe states that the term *brothers* is referring exclusively to believing Jews during the Tribulation. Wiersbe states the following regarding the term *brothers*: "Who are these people that the King dares to call 'My brethren'? It seems likely that they are the believing Jews from the Tribulation period. These are people who will hear the message of the 144,000 and trust Jesus Christ. Since these believing Jews will not receive the 'mark of the beast' (Revelation 13:16–17), they will be unable to buy or sell. How, then, can they survive? Through the loving care of the Gentiles who have trusted Christ and who care for His brethren." Wiersbe, W. W. (1996). *The Bible Exposition Commentary* (Matthew 25:31). Wheaton, IL: Victor Books.

Jesus personally identifies with the afflictions of His children. When one is persecuting you, for the cause of Christ, the person is actually persecuting Jesus. This is exemplified when Jesus spoke directly to Saul on his way to Damascus to attack believers.

> Acts 9:1–6: *"Now Saul, still breathing threats and murder against the disciples of the Lord, went to the high priest, and asked for letters from him to the synagogues at Damascus, so that if he found any belonging to the Way, both men and women, he might bring them bound to Jerusalem. As he was traveling, it happened that he was approaching Damascus, and suddenly a light from heaven flashed around him; and he fell to the ground and heard a voice saying to him, 'Saul, Saul, why are you persecuting Me?' And he said, 'Who are You, Lord?' And He said, 'I am Jesus whom you are persecuting, but get up and enter the city, and it will be told you what you must do.'"*

An accurate interpretation and application of Matthew 25:31-46 will not make you popular with non-believers, false disciples, and the social-gospel crowd. Those groups are interested in a gospel that recognizes their efforts at self-righteousness. Duane Litfin[73] accurately summarizes Matthew 25:31-46 when he writes:

> "When Jesus speaks there of 'the least of these my brothers,' he is not referring to just any poor person. There is no biblical warrant for supposing that people become Jesus' brothers or one of his "little ones" simply by becoming hungry, or thirsty, or impoverished, or incarcerated in prison (see also Matthew 12:49-50; 28:10; Hebrews 2:10-18). Nor does the Bible teach that such individuals somehow embody Jesus in the world. Jesus surely is embodied

---

[73] Dr. A. Duane Litfin served as the seventh president at Wheaton College.

in the world...in His followers (Colossians 2:19), His brothers, His disciples, His little ones who believe, even 'the least of them.'.... [B]y broadening it out to include all human suffering, however well-intentioned, does not merely miss Jesus's point; it undermines and falsifies it."[74]

A heart that is converted by Jesus Christ will result in good works for Christ's glory, not one's own glory. This is part of being a true disciple.

James 2:17-18: *"Even so faith, if it has no works, is dead, being by itself. But someone may well say, 'You have faith, and I have works; show me your faith without the works, and I will show you my faith by my works.'"*

The Lord Jesus is compassionate and generous. He is concerned about people's daily spiritual and physical needs (Matthew 9:36, 15:32).[75] The Lord will work through His people to minister to others, whether those in need are believers or not. This is God's common grace to all, which keeps us all from immediate justice the moment we sin. This concept is reflected in 1 Timothy 4:10 where it states, *"...because we have fixed our hope on the living God, who is the Savior of all men, especially of believers."* That

---

[74] Litfin, Duane (2012) *Words vs Deeds* p.192- 193 (Crossway Press).

[75] Scripture does not advocate throwing money at just *anyone* who says he is poor. Whether one is a Christian, or not, if he is healthy and refuses to work, the church is not to aimlessly waste resources on him.

> o 2 Thessalonians 3:10: *"For even when we were with you, we used to give you this order: if anyone is not willing to work, then he is not to eat, either."*
> o 1 Timothy 5:8: *"But if anyone does not provide for his own, and especially for those of his household, he has denied the faith and is worse than an unbeliever."*
> o Proverbs 23:21: *"For the heavy drinker and the glutton will come to poverty, And drowsiness will clothe one with rags."*

common grace also allows us to be the beneficiary of good things in this life, which we do not deserve. Christians are to be like their heavenly Father in showing grace since they have been shown infinite mercy and saving grace:

> **Matthew 5:44–45:** *"But I say to you, love your enemies and pray for those who persecute you, so that you may be sons of your Father who is in heaven; for He causes His sun to rise on the evil and the good, and sends rain on the righteous and the unrighteous."*

> **Acts 14:16-17:** *"In the generations gone by He permitted all the nations to go their own ways; and yet He did not leave Himself without witness, in that He did good and gave you rains from heaven and fruitful seasons, satisfying your hearts with food and gladness."*

We must have the same compassion as our Savior does, *"… for He Himself is kind to ungrateful and evil men."* (Luke 6:35). We are to do *"good to all"* but there is also a very special place for our brothers and sisters in Christ. Paul instructs this in:

> **Galatians 6:10:** *"…while we have opportunity, let us do good to all men, and especially to those who are of the household of the faith."*

> **1 Corinthians 12:26–27:** *"And if one member suffers, all the members suffer with it; if one member is honored, all the members rejoice with it. Now you are Christ's body, and individually members of it."*

John admonishes Christians to be there for fellow Christians in need:

> **1 John 3:16–17:** *"We know love by this, that He laid down His life for us; and we ought to lay down our lives for the brethren. But whoever has the world's*

> goods, and sees his brother in need and closes his
> heart against him, how does the love of God abide in
> him?"

We see the example of Paul sending financial support from the
Christians in Macedonia and Achaia, to the Christians in
Jerusalem (the saints): *"For Macedonia and Achaia have been
pleased to make a contribution for the poor among the saints in
Jerusalem."* (Romans 15:26).

In Acts, we see Christians giving according to their financial
ability. They were "determined" to provide relief to fellow
believers in Judea:

> Acts 11:29: *"And in the proportion that any of the
> disciples had means, each of them determined to send
> a contribution for the relief of the brethren living in
> Judea."*

The author of Hebrews writes of the great value of Christians
caring for one another when in prison for the gospel:

> Hebrews 13:1–3: *"Let love of the brethren continue.
> Do not neglect to show hospitality to strangers, for by
> this some have entertained angels without knowing it.
> Remember the prisoners, as though in prison with
> them, and those who are ill-treated, since you
> yourselves also are in the body."*

Paul also mentions the great value of Christian care when he was
in prison:

> 2 Timothy 1:16–18: *"The Lord grant mercy to the
> house of Onesiphorus, for he often refreshed me and
> was not ashamed of my chains; but when he was in
> Rome, he eagerly searched for me and found me— the
> Lord grant to him to find mercy from the Lord on that

day—and you know very well what services he rendered at Ephesus."

One should examine the list of causes that many in the fake commission / religious-left claim that they are zealous about. The list for some of those groups includes hunger, orphans, climate change, trafficking, income equality, social justice, gay rights, immigration and even abortion rights. There is one cause that is often at the bottom of the list (if it is mentioned at all) — *the persecution of fellow Christians for evangelizing the gospel.* The "Christian human rights" cause does not bring out the big corporate contributors and secular organizations to assist. The true Christians must champion the care and concern for all but *"especially to those who are of the household of the faith"* (Galatians 6:10).

In summary, neither Matthew 25:45, nor any other scripture in context supports the view that a person can be saved by earning one's own righteousness via acts of feeding, clothing or visiting prisoners. Aid to another's physical condition is not spiritually superior to preaching the gospel of Christ to that person. To claim that it is, rejects Jesus' example and results in practicing the fake commission. Jesus states clearly that He came to preach the gospel and pay the sacrifice for our sins on the cross.

Luke 4:43–44: *"But He said to them, 'I must preach the kingdom of God to the other cities also, for I was sent for this purpose.' So He kept on preaching in the synagogues of Judea."*

1 John 3:5: *"You know that He appeared in order to take away sins; and in Him there is no sin."*

THE
FAKE
COMMISSION

CHAPTER 6

WHAT IS THE GREAT COMMISSION?

"And Jesus came up and spoke to them, saying, 'All authority has been given to Me in heaven and on earth. [19] *Go therefore and make disciples of all the nations, baptizing them in the name of the Father and the Son and the Holy Spirit,* [20] *teaching them to observe all that I commanded you; and lo, I am with you always, even to the end of the age .'"* (Matthew 28:18-20).

"Therefore, to one who knows the right thing to do and does not do it, to him it is sin." (James 4:17).

Matthew 28:18-20 is commonly called The Great Commission. The Great Commission is often preached from the pulpit, but very neglected in practice. As mentioned previously, this occurs for many reasons such as being inadequately trained, to the worst scenario, not really being a Christian in the first place. We should take seriously the words of the English aristocrat C.T. Studd (1860-1931) who liquidated his wealth and his life to spread the gospel to the nations. Late in his life he said:

> "Too long have we been waiting for one another to begin! The time for waiting is past! ... Should such men as we fear? ...before the sleepy, lukewarm, faithless, namby-pamby Christian world, we will dare to trust our God,.... We will a thousand times sooner die trusting only in our God than live trusting in man. And when we come to this position the battle is already won, and the end of the glorious campaign in sight. We will have the real Holiness of God, not the sickly stuff of talk and dainty words and pretty thoughts; we will have the Masculine Holiness, one of daring faith and works for Jesus Christ." [76]

Let us examine The Great Commission set out in Matthew 28:18-20 in a verse-by-verse manner:

- **VERSES 18**: *"And Jesus came up and spoke to them, saying, 'All authority has been given to Me in heaven and on earth.'"*

Listen to the infinite magnitude of this statement! It is a statement that cannot be made by anyone except Almighty God, *"All authority has been given to Me in heaven and on earth."* One either believes this, or he does not. The statement of ultimate power and authority is set out right before He commands us to, *"make disciples of all the nations...."* The fact that He has ultimate and complete control of all things should annihilate any fears or misgivings we have about going out to, *"make disciples of all the nations...."*

When Jesus speaks of, *"All authority,"* He means, as God, He

---

[76] Grubb, Norman, 2001; *C.T. Studd: Cricketer and Pioneer*, p. 120-121 (CLC Publications).

controls all that was created, and all things are subject to His judgment. He has all authority to forgive sins and grant eternal life, as well as all authority to condemn to eternal damnation. Look at the following:

1. Jesus is the Creator of everything that exists:

    -   Colossians 1:16: *"For by Him all things were created, both in the heavens and on earth, visible and invisible, whether thrones or dominions or rulers or authorities—all things have been created through Him and for Him."*

2. Jesus is the Judge of everything that exists:

    -   John 5:22: *"For not even the Father judges anyone, but He has given all judgment to the Son,...."*

3. Jesus has all authority to forgive sins:

    -   Matthew 9:6: *"But so that you may know that the Son of Man has authority on earth to forgive sins."*

4. Jesus is the Resurrection, having all authority to give eternal life:

    -   John 11:25: *"Jesus said to her, 'I am the resurrection and the life; he who believes in Me will live even if he dies....'"*

    -   John 6:40: *"For this is the will of My Father, that everyone who beholds the Son and believes in Him will have eternal life, and I Myself will raise him up on the last day."*

5.   Jesus has all authority to condemn to hell:

- **Revelation 20:12–15:** *"And I saw the dead, the great and the small, standing before the throne, and books were opened; and another book was opened, which is the book of life; and the dead were judged from the things which were written in the books, according to their deeds. And the sea gave up the dead which were in it, and death and Hades gave up the dead which were in them; and they were judged, every one of them according to their deeds. Then death and Hades were thrown into the lake of fire. This is the second death, the lake of fire. And if anyone's name was not found written in the book of life, he was thrown into the lake of fire."*

- **Matthew 25:31–32, 41:** *"But when the Son of Man comes in His glory, and all the angels with Him, then He will sit on His glorious throne. All the nations will be gathered before Him; and He will separate them from one another, as the shepherd separates the sheep from the goats…. ⁴¹Then He will also say to those on His left, 'Depart from Me, accursed ones, into the eternal fire which has been prepared for the devil and his angels….'"*

Our Lord told us ahead of time that He is sending us out as defenseless sheep among ravenous wolves whose nature is to

attack us. Yet, He is in such ultimate control He tells us we are not to be concerned or fearful of being maligned, hated, disowned by family, arrested, beaten, or even murdered (e.g. Matthew 10:25, 21-22, 17-19, 28).

> Matthew 10:16–39: *"Behold, I send you out as sheep in the midst of wolves; so be shrewd as serpents and innocent as doves. [17] But beware of men, for they will hand you over to the courts and scourge you in their synagogues; [18] and you will even be brought before governors and kings for My sake, as a testimony to them and to the Gentiles. [19] But when they hand you over, do not worry about how or what you are to say; for it will be given you in that hour what you are to say. [20] For it is not you who speak, but it is the Spirit of your Father who speaks in you. [21]Brother will betray brother to death, and a father his child; and children will rise up against parents and cause them to be put to death. [22] You will be hated by all because of My name, but it is the one who has endured to the end who will be saved. [23] But whenever they persecute you in one city, flee to the next; for truly I say to you, you will not finish going through the cities of Israel until the Son of Man comes. [24] A disciple is not above his teacher, nor a slave above his master. [25] It is enough for the disciple that he become like his teacher, and the slave like his master. If they have called the head of the house Beelzebul, how much more will they malign the members of his household! [26]Therefore do not fear them, for there is nothing concealed that will not be revealed, or hidden that will not be known. [27] What I tell you in the darkness, speak in the light; and what you hear whispered in your ear, proclaim upon the housetops. [28] Do not fear those who kill the body but are unable to kill the soul; but rather fear Him who is able to destroy both soul and body in hell. [29]Are not two sparrows sold for a cent? And yet not one of them will fall to the ground apart from your*

Father. ³⁰But the very hairs of your head are all numbered. ³¹ So do not fear; you are more valuable than many sparrows .³² Therefore everyone who confesses Me before men, I will also confess him before My Father who is in heaven. ³³ But whoever denies Me before men, I will also deny him before My Father who is in heaven. ³⁴ Do not think that I came to bring peace on the earth; I did not come to bring peace, but a sword. ³⁵ For I came to set a man against his father, and a daughter against her mother, and a daughter-in-law against her mother-in-law; ³⁶ and a man's enemies will be the members of his household. ³⁷ He who loves father or mother more than Me is not worthy of Me; and he who loves son or daughter more than Me is not worthy of Me. ³⁸ And he who does not take his cross and follow after Me is not worthy of Me. ³⁹ He who has found his life will lose it, and he who has lost his life for My sake will find it."

The reality is many modern U.S. evangelicals will appear bold when talking about *standing up for Christ*, but cower when confronted with a *costly stand* for Him. I watched as a church terminated a very fruitful mission project for the youth to a *risky* area, even though the youth and their parents were fully aware of the risks and assumed those risks. The church stated it wanted to assure no youth would get hurt and more specifically assure that the church would not possibly get sued. (Sued? Property loss *or* reaching the lost?) The decision may have made sense from a defensive corporate viewpoint, but that is not the Biblical perspective or Jesus' command. Christ does not call us to self-preservation or property protection above the call of true discipleship and reaching the lost: *"For whoever wishes to save his life will lose it; but whoever loses his life for My sake will find it"* (Matthew 16:25); *"So then, none of you can be My disciple who does not give up all his own possessions."* (Luke 14:33). A couple of weeks later, during the Sunday service, the same church sang a praise song about its unwavering devotion to Christ that contained the following words: *"If this life I lose, I will follow* you."[77] Obviously many find it easier to sing of their loyalty to Christ than to live it. We must encourage each other that the standard is scripture and not society.

> **Hebrews 10:34:** *"For you showed sympathy to the prisoners and accepted joyfully the seizure of your property, knowing that you have for yourselves a better possession and a lasting one."*

The unspoken view in much of the church is that, "I am more than willing to send a check to the mission field, but I am not willing to let Christ send me." This is tragic, and a denial of the faith. I can already hear the disdain by some for the previous sentence (i.e. that it is *a denial of the faith*). The offended will proudly tell you how they stand for the faith and immediately begin reciting orthodox tenants of the faith they claim to believe. They do not realize, *"...the kingdom of God does not consist in words but in power."* 1 Corinthians 4:20. They also forget the demons *fearfully* believe orthodox tenants of the faith ... *they just do not obey them.*

> **James 2:19-20:** *"You believe that God is one. You do well; the demons also believe, and shudder. [20] But are you willing to recognize, you foolish fellow, that faith without works is useless?"*

Many are those who are content to raise their hands during worship, or to get out their notepad for the sermon, but are not willing to obey the commands of Christ. Why are they comfortable this way? The answer is simple: This is the acceptable standard for most of the modern church. This may be acceptable for church membership and leadership, but it is not the Christianity Jesus set forth when He said: *"If you love Me, you will keep My commandments."* (John 14:15).

---

[77] *I Will Follow* by Chris Tomlin.

I have been involved with evangelism for more than 35 years and it is my hope that some might learn from my experiences. Specifically, I believe there are two lessons to keep in mind when engaging in true evangelism:

The first lesson is not to be surprised at the fierceness of opposition you will face when you are involved in *true evangelism*. The attacks will occur from both inside and outside the visible church. The most discouraging attacks will be from those within the church. Sometimes it may be false-brethren (cf. Galatians 2:4). Don't be discouraged; remember that the Lord gave us Judas as the example of *the false* functioning (with great camouflage) among the elect. Other times it may be spiritually immature or sinning brothers/sisters leading the attack. You need to forgive all and go on. Do not give the devil a foothold by being arrogant or bitter. Remember that we all regret some of our own unscriptural or fleshly opinions, decisions and actions that have hindered the gospel.

Do not become distracted by other's criticisms and slanders. Paul himself experienced the call of God to effective service while simultaneously facing strong opposition by others: "*...for a wide door for effective service has opened to me, and there are many adversaries....*" (1 Corinthians 16:9). Understand that in most cases, you will never satisfy your detractors by trying to answer all their *concerns*. It becomes a shell-game of sorts; if you answer one question well, you will be rewarded with two new *concerns* demanded to be addressed.

One church leader told an evangelist that he does not engage in door-to-door evangelism because it is not effective. (I am confident it is more effective than sitting at home watching T.V.) These types of excuses have an appearance of wisdom, but they hide deeper issues we all need to deal with. I would ask such a man this question: "If it is so ineffective, why does every politician (whether running for dogcatcher or president) believe that door-to-door campaigns are central to an election strategy?" The reality is that door-to-door evangelism provides personal contact with people who may never come to your church building. When you go to a person's front door, the person you meet feels comfortable and in control of the location. If he has no interest in talking to you, he will ask you to leave. On the other hand, many will appreciate that you cared enough to actually come to them. Especially when you do not look like a white-shirt / black-tie clone from a 1950's sci-fi movie.

During a two-week time-period in the summer of 2014, I experienced door-to-door evangelism in my community, and hut-to-hut evangelism in a jungle area of Africa. The Lord was gracious. Despite very different environments, cultures and socioeconomic status, we were welcomed by many we visited, and we were able to effectively share the gospel.[78] My point is, do not spend a lot of time addressing other's complaints when you are trying to Biblically reach others for Christ. If a person has *no interest* in putting himself in an uncomfortable situation to evangelize, you will waste time trying to convince him, and he will become embittered against you. Be gracious and stay focused on the call you have been given (Matthew 28:19-20).[79] Remember that in the end, you serve and answer to an audience of ONE...the Lord. Despite the disappointment, discouragement and loneliness, do not let your heart be troubled. There is a great peace the Holy Spirit gives to those who are obedient to the will of God: *"Have I not commanded you? Be strong and courageous! Do not tremble or*

---

[78] There were a few times in Africa that small children were scared when they saw us stop at their home. Their parents would laugh and explain that the child had never before seen a muzungu (white person). We would then be invited to sit and talk about the things of God. Often when we were leaving, they would tell us that we "were most welcome" to come back anytime. Remember, the gospel has no boundaries.

[79] Nehemiah 6:2–4: *"...then Sanballat and Geshem sent a message to me, saying, "Come, let us meet together at Chephirim in the plain of Ono." But they were planning to harm me.* [3] *So I sent messengers to them, saying, "I am doing a great work and I cannot come down. Why should the work stop while I leave it and come down to you?"* [4] *They sent messages to me four times in this manner, and I answered them in the same way."*

be dismayed, for the Lord your God is with you wherever you go." (Joshua 1:9).

A preacher once told the story of a Christian youth who was busy evangelizing his community. The youth would respectfully speak to others of the judgment of hell, repentance, Christ's resurrection and salvation only by faith in Christ's death on the cross as the payment for sin. This did not settle well with a proud church elder who told the young man his "negative message" about hell and telling people they were sinners, was giving the church a "bad name." He went on to tell the young man: "If you really need to say something, then tell people there is a wonderful and happy life for them if they would just *ask Jesus into their heart...*then leave it at that!" The church elder could see the young man was clearly unpersuaded. The elder became angrier and wagged his finger at the young man and said, "Your message has set back evangelism in this community by 10 years!" Finally, he could see that he made his point. The young man dropped his head and said, "I am very sorry to hear that — I was hoping to set it back 2,000 years."

J. C. Ryle addressed the issue of complainers in the church when he stated:

> "The spirit of these narrow-minded fault-finders is unhappily all too common. Their followers and successors are to be found in every part of Christ's visible church. There is never any lack of people who decry what they call 'extremes' in religion, and are incessantly recommending what they term 'moderation' in the service of Christ. If someone devotes time, money and affection to the pursuit of worldly things, they do not blame him. If he gives himself up to the service of money, pleasure or politics, they find no fault. But if the same person devotes himself and all he has to Christ, they can scarcely find words to express their sense of his folly. 'He is beside himself.' 'He is out of his mind.' 'He is a

fanatic.' 'He is an enthusiast.' 'He is too righteous.'' He is an extremist.' In short, they regard it as 'waste.' Let charges like these not disturb us if we hear them made against us because we strive to serve Christ. Let us bear them patiently, and remember that they are as old as Christianity itself. Let us pity those who make such charges against believers. They show plainly that they have no sense of obligation to Christ. A cold heart makes a slow hand. Once a person understands the sinfulness of sin and the mercy of Christ in dying for them, they will never think anything too good or too costly to give to Christ. They will rather feel, 'How can I repay the Lord for all his goodness to me?' (Psalm 116:12). They will fear wasting their time, talents, money, affections on the things of this world. They will not be afraid of wasting them on the Savior. They will fear going to extremes about business, money, politics or pleasure, but will not be afraid of doing too much for Christ."[80]

The second lesson to learn, is that deep down, most of those in the church pews do not really want any part of suffering persecution for the sake of the gospel. To avoid this persecution, they default from the clear commands regarding evangelism and discipleship and create their own user-friendly version of evangelism. The excuse called *friendship evangelism* is the technique of choice for most Christians who are untrained, fearful, immature, or false-christians within the church. *Friendship evangelism*, in its simplest form, means you act real nice to someone so that over time the person will trust you and like you. After you have the person's attention, *some year* down the road [hopefully before either of you die, move away, or decide to end the friendship] you will have impressed him so much he will ask you why you are so *nice and happy*. You then tell him it is because

---

[80] Ryle, J. C. (1993). *Mark*. Crossway Classic Commentaries (pp. 220–221). Wheaton, IL: Crossway Books.

you are a Christian and then you either invite him to church or tell him he can be *happy too* if he *asks Jesus into his heart.*

Obviously there are different slants on *friendship evangelism,* but the unspoken technique remains the same: I am holding back the truth of the gospel until someone is so impressed with *me* that I have earned the right to be listened to. Please do not misunderstand me. Obviously, scripture teaches that all believers are to live godly lives before unbelievers, but a godly life is to be lived out of love for Christ and not to escape the responsibility of telling others the truth of the gospel. In addition, it is God who opens their eyes to be saved. If I simply win someone over to try my lifestyle, I have made him a disciple of me and not Christ. Worse yet, the person will think he has tried Christianity when he was never even saved. Again, God has chosen to proclaim His message through the, *"foolishness of preaching."*

> 1 Corinthians 1:21: *"For since in the wisdom of God the world through its wisdom did not come to know God, God was well-pleased through the foolishness of the message preached to save those who believe."*

> Romans 10:13–15: *"…Whoever will call on the name of the Lord will be saved.* [14] *How then will they call on Him in whom they have not believed? How will they believe in Him whom they have not heard? And how will they hear without a preacher?* [15] *How will they preach unless they are sent? Just as it is written, 'How beautiful are the feet of those who bring good news of good things!'"*

The true gospel informs the (friend, enemy, family member or stranger you just met) that he is a sinner for whom hell awaits unless he repents and believes in Christ's atoning death on the cross as the only basis for him to be forgiven. Understand that when you do this (via conversation, gospel tract, etc.) some of the *friendship evangelism* people will berate you for *turning people away* and being *unloving.* They have this viewpoint because they are ultimately concerned about how they appear in the public's eye and not how they appear through the eyes of Christ.

I have a friend who is a missionary to unreached people groups in South America. Recently, he was sent by a mission organization to another country to check on a particular missionary's progress. My friend observed that the missionary would periodically build stuff or work on small projects for some around the area. One thing was always missing—there was no sharing of the true gospel. People were just left thinking the "missionary guy" was nice.

One day my friend was at a home where the missionary was doing home improvements and he finally asked him: "When are you going to tell them about Christ?" The missionary responded by saying he was, "focusing on building relationships." Exasperated, my friend stated, "You have been doing that for 20 years! If you won't preach, I will." He then went on to tell the family about Christ. He also told me that the "so-called missionary" was offended by his impromptu preaching to the family. My friend also told me that over the years he has run into many "occupational missionaries." He uses that term to describe those who live in a foreign country, have good funding from U.S. Christians, engage in some social issues in their neighborhood, and rarely, if ever preach the gospel outside a church building.[81]

---

[81] My friend's comments should not go unheeded. The presentation of a few photos and a couple of good stories is not a sufficient audit of a missionary's work. Likewise raw numbers may not tell the whole story either. My friend has confronted other *missionaries* who have misled supporters by telling stories of events "out on the field" which were actually my friend's story. What is sad is that the *"missionary"* stole the story from a ministry event he had nothing to do with to impress his supporters.

When determining who to support and at what level, listen to the missionary's heart, ask the hard questions and pray. Ask the person if he has regularly scheduled evangelism outreaches. What does the missionary's typical week-schedule (Sunday–Saturday) look like? How often does he preach on the weekend? Is the missionary actively discipling other Christians? How many Bible studies does he teach during the week? What does he do for his own daily devotions and personal study? Ask the

THE FAKE COMMISSION

Scripture does not tell me to withhold the gospel from others until I have proved myself either winsome/cute/smart or trusted

missionary to pretend that you are a non-believer, and then ask him to share the gospel with you. Missionaries you support should be very concerned about the lost state of those they are around. They must have a proven track record of spreading the gospel where they lived before being sent somewhere else. Make sure your missionary does not call "spreading the gospel" engaging in the *fake commission*.

One last issue, ask how much support he receives from other churches and individuals each month and how is it budgeted? In a *few* situations you may be surprised at the abundance of finances taken in each month. A missionary told me about another missionary he knows, who owns two homes in the city of the mission location. One home is a nice, average-style home. The second is a luxurious home/mansion with a swimming pool and hot tub. He told me how the missionary misleads donors who visit him. When visitors arrive, the missionary will live in the average-sized home and not tell them about his luxury home. Once the visitors leave, he moves back into his luxury home. A comfortable home is not the problem—the deception regarding your sacrifice and lack of funds is. It is very unlikely that his donors are interested in financing a luxurious life — and he obviously understands that.

Do not let "American guilt" keep you from inquiring. By "American guilt" I mean the view that since you work hard and have a comfortable living, how dare you ask these questions since the person gave up so much to be on the mission field! It is true that *many* missionaries have given up everything to faithfully serve God, but some did not. The false missionaries are using the mission field to live life in a foreign land and escape responsibility and accountability. Just as an employer would not pay employees who will not produce, I am not going to give money to "further the gospel" to those who have little interest in doing the work. Just calling yourself a "missionary" does not make you one. The reality is that *unaccountable giving takes money away from true missionaries.*

True missionaries deserve our strong support and like a godly elder, true missionaries are: *".... considered worthy of double honor, especially those who work hard at preaching and teaching. For the Scripture says, 'You shall not muzzle the ox while he is threshing,' and 'The laborer is worthy of his wages.'"* (1 Timothy 5:17–18). These excellent missionaries, who labor hard preaching the gospel and truly engaging in the Great Commission, must be magnanimously encouraged and *"You will do well to send them on their way in a manner worthy of God."* (3 John 6).

enough to *earn* the right to tell them. We are commanded to go and tell the truth in love, leaving the results with God. The saving message of the cross stands on the merits of Christ, not me. D. Martin Lloyd-Jones stated:

> "Evangelism must start with the holiness of God, the sinfulness of man, the demands of the law, and the eternal consequences of evil."[82]

I have had many meaningful conversations about the gospel with complete strangers. If you simply talk to them, you find most people are very concerned about what happens to them after they die. Maybe you struggle with talking to people. If so, give out high-quality tracts that accurately state the gospel. Hand them to the clerk at the check-out or drive-through or wherever you go. After you do it, you will wonder why you disregarded these opportunities in the past.

One tract I have found well received is the evangelism "bookmark" we created. In just a few years, tens of thousands are in print and have been used very effectively in the U.S. and other countries like Uganda, Mexico, Guatemala and Jamaica. They are a high-quality bookmark that accurately presents the gospel. You can view them and receive 25 of them free by going to our website (request either English or Spanish). The QR code for the bookmarks is:

The direct webpage is:

http://CrossCenteredMissions.org/evangelismresources/gospelbookmark/

---

[82] Lloyd-Jones, Martin. *Studies in the Sermon on the Mount"*

In summary, keep a correct perspective in reference to the fear of man, compared to the fear of God. Paul understood that: *"Therefore, knowing the fear of the Lord, we persuade men..."* (2 Corinthians 5:11). Realize that the day will come when all mankind will fear the Living God and bow before His majesty and authority.

> Philippians 2:9–11: *"For this reason also, God highly exalted Him, and bestowed on Him the name which is above every name, [10] so that at the name of Jesus every knee will bow, of those who are in heaven and on earth and under the earth, [11] and that every tongue will confess that Jesus Christ is Lord, to the glory of God the Father."*

The point to take away from Matthew 28:18 is that our Lord is in complete control of ALL THINGS. Since He has ABSOLUTE AUTHORITY, we have no need to fear man when going out to spread the gospel. Isaiah 2:22: *"Stop regarding man, whose breath of life is in his nostrils; For why should he be esteemed?"*

John Piper writes in his book, *Don't Waste Your Life*, a section on what our view of risk and danger should be in service to God. He points out that risk includes the potential loss of money, reputation, health, life, and possibly *endangering other people* (p. 79). Piper goes on to say:

> "Why is there such a thing as risk? Because there is such a thing as ignorance. If there were no ignorance there would be no risk. Risk is possible because we don't know how things will turn out. This means that God can take no risks! He knows the outcome of all His choices before they happen....[b]ut not so with us. We are not God, we are ignorant. We don't know what will happen tomorrow. He does not tell us in detail what He intends to do tomorrow or five years from now. Evidently God intends for us to live and act in ignorance and in uncertainty about the

outcome of our actions.... Therefore, risk is woven into the fabric of our finite lives. We cannot avoid risk even if we want to. Ignorance and uncertainty about tomorrow is our native air. All of our plans for tomorrow's activities can be shattered by a thousand unknowns whether we stay at home under the covers or ride the freeways. One of my aims is to explode the myth of safety and to somehow deliver you from the enchantment of security. Because it's a mirage. It doesn't exist. Every direction you turn there are unknowns and things beyond your control.... The way I hope to explode the myth of safety and to disenchant you with the mirage of security is simply to go to the Bible and show that it is right to risk for the cause of Christ, ...and not to is to waste your life."[83]

Piper then points to the Apostle Paul as an example. Paul was told by the Holy Spirit that, *"in every city... imprisonment and afflictions await me."* (Acts 20:23). Read about those tribulations in 2 Corinthians 11:24-28. Piper concludes by stating:

"Every day [Paul] risked his life for the cause of God.... He had two choices: waste his life or live with risk. And he answered this choice clearly: *"But I do not consider my life of any account as dear to myself, so that I may finish my course and the ministry which I received from the Lord Jesus, to testify solemnly of the gospel of the grace of God."*

MacArthur states the following about persecution and fear of death:

"The worst that can happen to a believer suffering unjustly is death, and that is the best that can

---

[83] Piper, John, *"Don't Waste Your Life."* p. 80-81 (Crossway Books, 2003).

happen because death means the complete and final end of all sins. If the Christian is armed with the goal of being delivered from sin, and that goal is achieved through his death, the threat and experience of death is precious (cf. Romans 7:5, 18; 1 Corinthians 1:21; 15:42,49). Moreover, the greatest weapon that the enemy has against the Christian, the threat of death, is not effective."[84]

In summing up this concept of *safety* and our service to God, David Jeremiah said it well when he pointed out that,

"...a man of God, in the will of God, *is immortal,* until his work on earth is done."[85]

- **Matthew 28:19 (first part of the verse):** *"Go therefore and make disciples of all the nations...."*

It is clear we are to *go* make disciples.[86] Where are we to go? The answer is clear—we are to go throughout the entire world. Mark 16:15 states, *"And He said to them, 'Go into all the world and preach the gospel to all creation.'"* I have heard many a pastor

---

[84] MacArthur, John Jr., Ed.) *The MacArthur Study Bible.* 1997 (electronic ed.) (1 Peter 4:1). Nashville, TN: Word Publications.

[85] Jeremiah, David, *"The Handwriting on the Wall: Secrets from the Prophecies of Daniel."* p.127 Thomas Nelson, 1992.

[86] Grammatical arguments have been put forward by some that πορευθέντες should be translated as "having gone" or "as you are going." Such translations, however, cause renowned Greek scholar Daniel Wallace to disagree. Wallace states that the mistranslation mistakenly turns "the Great Commission into the Great Suggestion!" Wallace, Daniel B. Greek *Grammar Beyond the Basics: An Exegetical Syntax of the New Testament with Scripture, Subject, and Greek Word Indexes.* Grand Rapids, MI: Zondervan, 1996, 645. In summary disciples of Jesus are to go and make disciples—the Great Commission still stands – go!

comfort a congregation by downplaying this command; inferring that they are doing all the Lord wants of them by being good people on the job and serving in the church. The pastor will often conclude by saying that, "we need people to stay here to make money to send others; after all, *we can't all go*." We can't? It is more accurate to say that we choose not to. Yes, it is true, you are to be a good witness where you are planted (that assumes you are actually witnessing) but that does not excuse you from going out. Nowhere does scripture tell us that *only* certain people are to make money to pay for missions and, only certain others (without much money) are the ones to go. Whether it is long-term or short-term, near or far, we are all to go,...and help others to go, and pray for more to go! "*...The harvest is plentiful, but the workers are few. Therefore beseech the Lord of the harvest to send out workers into His harvest.*" (Matthew 9:37–38). If you do that, I should warn you: Driving the finest cars available may not occur during your life as you finance yourself and others on the mission field.

Another line you will hear from some of the religious while they question/discourage you from going out: "*There is plenty of work to do right here in our community. Why do you need to go to _____?* (Fill in the blank of the mission location or country.) If the questioners were busy doing real evangelism in their community, the *work* they claim to be so *concerned* about would have been done long ago. The point is clear—Jesus tells us to go, and *go we must*, whether it makes sense to family or so-called church people.

The martyr Jim Elliot believed he was called to be a missionary to the Quichuas Indians.[87] Some people in the church tried to dissuade him with various reasons including that it was too risky. These type of subtle attacks on the mind, by the enemy and misguided church people, must be countered by God's Word! Elliot addressed these counter-calls when he wrote:

---

[87] Quichuas is a language of indigenous people of South America. There are Indians who speak this language and live in Ecuador.

"Consider the call from the Throne above, 'Go ye,'
and from round about, 'Come over and help us,' and
even the call from the damned souls below, 'Send
Lazarus to my brothers, that they come not to this
place.' Impelled, then, by these voices, I dare not
stay home while Quichuas perish. So what if the
well-fed church in the homeland needs stirring?
They have the Scriptures, Moses and the Prophets,
and a whole lot more. Their condemnation is written
on their bank books and in the dust on their Bible
covers. American believers have sold their lives to
the service of Mammon, and God has His rightful
way of dealing with those who succumb to the spirit
of Laodicea."[88]

As you grow in Christ, your love for Christ will give you a
vision much bigger than your little area of life. You will truly
develop a heart for missions and recognize some of the following
seven changes occurring in your life:

1) Your heart will stir for those who do not know Christ
    because you really believe that the unsaved are heading to
    a fiery hell for all eternity.

    Revelation 20:11–15: *"Then I saw a great white
    throne and Him who sat upon it, from whose
    presence earth and heaven fled away, and no*

---

[88] Elliot, Elisabeth, 1979, *Shadow of the Almighty: The Life and Testament
of Jim Elliot*, p. 132 HarperCollins.

Extra note: Jim Elliot makes reference to different Bible verses in the
quote above. "...to Throne above, *'Go ye"*– (Matthew 28:18-20); "...from
round about, *'Come over and help us,'"*– (Acts 16:9); "...even the call from the
damned souls below, *'Send Lazarus to my brothers, that they come not
to this place.'"*– (Luke 16:23–31); "...*They have the Scriptures, Moses and the
Prophets,...*"– (Luke 16:29); "American believers have sold their lives to the
service of Mammon...."– (Luke 16:13); "His rightful way of dealing with
those who succumb to the spirit of Laodicea."– (Revelation 3:14–16).

place was found for them. [12] *And I saw the dead, the great and the small, standing before the throne, and books were opened; and another book was opened, which is the book of life; and the dead were judged from the things which were written in the books, according to their deeds.* [13] *And the sea gave up the dead which were in it, and death and Hades gave up the dead which were in them; and they were judged, every one of them according to their deeds.* [14] *Then death and Hades were thrown into the lake of fire. This is the second death, the lake of fire.* [15] *And if anyone's name was not found written in the book of life, he was thrown into the lake of fire."*

2) You will have a heart for those serving on the mission field.

> **Colossians 2:5:** *"For even though I am absent in body, nevertheless I am with you in spirit, rejoicing to see your good discipline and the stability of your faith in Christ."*

3) Your heart will skip when you hear on Sunday morning that someone is giving a mission report. (Those without a heart for missions will roll their eyes and think, "what a bore," or that the missionary just wants their money.) You will be excited to hear what *"God had done."*

> **Acts 14:27:** *"When they had arrived and gathered the church together, they began to report all things that God had done with them and how He had opened a door of faith to the Gentiles."*

4) You will look for ways to help missionaries with their work and serve them.

Philippians 4:16–18: "*...for even in Thessalonica you sent a gift more than once for my needs. [17] Not that I seek the gift itself, but I seek for the profit which increases to your account. [18] But I have received everything in full and have an abundance; I am amply supplied, having received from Epaphroditus what you have sent, a fragrant aroma, an acceptable sacrifice, well-pleasing to God.*"

5) You will pray for those who are persecuted for the gospel.

1 Corinthians 12:26: "*And if one member suffers, all the members suffer with it; if one member is honored, all the members rejoice with it.*"

Colossians 4:18: "*I, Paul, write this greeting with my own hand. Remember my imprisonment...*"

6) You will pray for the Lord to add workers to the mission field.

Matthew 9:37–38: "*Then He said to His disciples, 'The harvest is plentiful, but the workers are few. [38] Therefore beseech the Lord of the harvest to send out workers into His harvest.'*"

7) Finally, you will go yourself! It may be nearby or far away; it may be long-term or very short-term; it may be a big work or a small work; *but you will go and continue to go.* On the mission you will experience trials, tribulations, persecution along with spiritual fruit and GREAT JOY!

Now that we have established we are to go, what are we to accomplish? Jesus said we are to, "*make disciples of all the nations,"* (not simply build and repair stuff). A disciple is a learner/follower. We are to make disciples of Jesus Christ, and not of ourselves or our church denomination. It is very unbecoming when those in the church try to create subgroups/groupies around a leader.

> **1 Corinthians 1:12–13:** *"Now I mean this, that each one of you is saying, 'I am of Paul,' and 'I of Apollos,' and 'I of Cephas,' and 'I of Christ.' 13 Has Christ been divided? Paul was not crucified for you, was he? Or were you baptized in the name of Paul?"*

A man of God will use his influence to constantly point people to Christ and not himself. Paul said in 1 Corinthians 11:1: *"Be imitators of me, just as I also am of Christ."*

- **Matthew 28:19 (second part of the verse):** *"...baptizing them in the name of the Father and the Son and the Holy Spirit...."*

We also are to see that the new disciples in Christ are baptized. I am always highly suspect of people who say they are Christians but will not be baptized. Such a view is rebellion against the words of Christ (Matthew 28:19). Baptism is expected for those who believe unto salvation.

> **Acts 8:36–38:** *"As they went along the road they came to some water; and the eunuch said, 'Look! Water! What prevents me from being baptized?' 37 [And Philip said, 'If you believe with all your heart, you may.' And he answered and said, 'I believe that Jesus Christ is the Son of God.'] 38 And he ordered the chariot to stop; and they both went down into the water, Philip as well as the eunuch, and he baptized him."*

Baptism is to be done in the name of the Holy Trinity (*"the name of the Father and the Son and the Holy Spirit...."*). This makes clear the error of "oneness theology." Oneness theology (also known as, "Jesus only," or "modalism")[89] denies the fundamental doctrine of the Trinity and claims you must baptize in the name of *Jesus only* (directly contrary to the words of Jesus in Matthew 28:19).

Being baptized into the body of Christ is not a magical rite obtained through a special man with special water. Remember, baptism does not save you, only faith in Christ can do that. R. C. Sproul states it this way:

> "Baptism was instituted by Christ and is to be administered in the name of the Father, Son, and Holy Spirit. The outward sign does not automatically or magically convey the realities that are signified. For example, though baptism signifies regeneration, or rebirth, it does not automatically convey rebirth. The power of baptism is not in the water but in the power of God."[90]

Just as some make the great error in believing the ritual of water baptism instills eternal salvation, others error in thinking water baptism is insignificant. Water baptism is very important for the Christian. During water baptism, an individual publicly identifies himself with Christ and the body of Christ (i.e. the church). It outwardly symbolizes the spiritual baptism/conversion that has taken place inwardly. (See 1 Corinthians 12:13, Romans 6:2-11.) You will often hear an evangelist call people to the front of the church or alter to be publically identified with Christ. That is

---

[89] "The church has rejected the heresies of 'modalism' and 'tritheism'. 'Modalism' denies the distinction of persons within the Godhead, claiming that Father, Son, and Holy Spirit are just ways in which God expresses Himself. 'Tritheism,' on the other hand, falsely declares that there are three beings who together make up God." Sproul, R. C., *Essential Truths of the Christian Faith*, Wheaton, Ill.: Tyndale House (1996, c1992).

[90] Sproul, R. C. (1996) *Essential Truths of the Christian Faith; #80 Baptism*, Wheaton, Ill.: Tyndale House.

fine, but baptism is the Biblical form of public identification with Christ. Acts 2:41: "*So then, those who had received his word were baptized; and that day there were added about three thousand souls.*"

- <u>Matthew 28:20</u> (first part of the verse): "*...teaching them to observe all that I commanded you....*"

The obedient Christian equips new disciples who have come to faith in Christ: "*...teaching them to observe all that I commanded you....*" Jesus did not say to go and teach them all the great *life lessons* you have learned from your church. He told us to teach them what He *commanded*. Obedience to Christ is a manifestation of the converted: "*If you love Me, you will keep* My *commandments.*" (John 14:15). The commandments of God are summed up by our Lord:

> Matthew 22:36–39: "*Teacher, which is the great commandment in the Law?*" *37And He said to him, "You shall love the Lord your God with all your heart, and with all your soul, and with all your mind." 38This is the great and foremost commandment. 39"The second is like it, 'You shall love your neighbor as yourself.'*

Some have tried to twist the teachings of Christ into a life-enhancement program. This view sees the gospel as helping people to improve their marriage, get a promotion at work, and be better people. The true gospel reconciles sinful man to the perfect God. Man escapes the well-deserved judgment of hell through faith in Jesus Christ's substitutionary death on the cross. The believer is set free from sin and death and can live joyfully for the glory of God. John 10:10: "*...I came that they may have life, and have it abundantly.*"

Once a person comes to the revelation of what Christ has done for him, he is never the same. Nothing else matters but The King and His Kingdom.

> Matthew 13:44–46: *"The kingdom of heaven is like a treasure hidden in the field, which a man found and hid again; and from joy over it he goes and sells all that he has and buys that field. 45 Again, the kingdom of heaven is like a merchant seeking fine pearls, 46 and upon finding one pearl of great value, he went and sold all that he had and bought it."*

- <u>Matthew 28:20</u> (second part of the verse): *"...and lo, I am with you always, even to the end of the age."*

The last section in Matthew 28:20 sets out the promise of comfort and security in Christ... to the very end. As some writers have pointed out, our Lord calls us *friends* in John 15:15; our Lord calls us *brothers* in Hebrews 2:11; but what is even more awesome is that He tells us He is *Immanuel—GOD WITH US...."* (Matthew 1:23). Yes, He is God with us...*"always, even to the end of the age."*

Do not miss that Matthew 28:18-20 is composed of an *introduction*, a *command*, and a *conclusion*. The *introduction* starts with Jesus setting forth His complete sovereignty over all that exists when He states, *"All authority has been given to Me in heaven and on earth."* The *conclusion* states the fact of His constant care and comfort: *"and lo, I am with you always, even to the end of the age."* Note that in between the introduction and conclusion is the *command*: *"Go therefore and make disciples of all the nations, baptizing them in the name of the Father and the Son and the Holy Spirit, 20 teaching them to observe all that I commanded you...."* It could not be made clearer: God is in complete control, and He is with us to the end, so we can confidently go out and spread the gospel and not be hindered by selfish concerns. Will you obey the

Lord? I hope so. Let us begin to learn how to share the gospel with others.

THE FAKE COMMISSION

CHAPTER 7

HOW DO I GET STARTED EFFECTIVELY EVANGELIZING?

> Jesus said to His disciples: *"We must work the works of Him who sent Me as long as it is day; night is coming when no one can work."* (John 9:4).

What should one do to effectively evangelize? The answer is simple: While you are still alive and able, declare the truth of the gospel and engage in good works to glorify God. How do you execute that? Over the years I have experienced many different evangelism programs. During my life I have had the privilege of sharing the gospel with friends in high school, engaging in open-air preaching at universities, preaching in churches, handing out tracts and Bibles and preaching in cities both in and outside the U.S. As I mentioned previously, when engaging in *real* evangelism, you must understand that you will not be warmly received by a majority of the crowd. Worse yet, you will probably not be warmly received by even a *minority* of the crowd. You should not take that personally. Look to Jesus' own words about how many would receive it. When He was asked how many would be saved, Jesus used the word *"few."*

Matthew 7:14: *"For the gate is small and the way is narrow that leads to life, and there are few who find it."*

Matthew 22:14: *"For many are called, but few are chosen."*

Other than the "few" how will the rest respond? They will not remain ambivalent regarding Jesus. If you share with them that God's Word says they are guilty of sin, many will resist that truth. As they fight against their conscience, they will direct their attack against you. You can explain that you too have sinned many times, and are also in great need of forgiveness, but it will not calm down the unrepentant and self-righteous. For some reason, the Christian thinks that since he is out doing God's work, everything should work out good, without any problems and "he will be blessed!" Ultimately, it will work out good, and he is blessed! Just do not be surprised by the trials along the way. The apostle Peter also reminds us of this:

1 Peter 4:12–14: *"Beloved, do not be surprised at the fiery ordeal among you, which comes upon you for your testing, as though some strange thing were happening to you; but to the degree that you share the sufferings of Christ, keep on rejoicing, so that also at the revelation of His glory you may rejoice with exultation. If you are reviled for the name of Christ, you are blessed, because the Spirit of glory and of God rests on you."*

Jesus makes it clear that you will be blessed!

Luke 6:22–23: *"Blessed are you when men hate you, and ostracize you, and insult you, and scorn your name as evil, for the sake of the Son of Man. "Be glad in that day and leap for joy, for behold, your reward is great in heaven. For in the same way their fathers used to treat the prophets."*

The Apostle Paul, the premier evangelist, also experienced severe trials when sharing the gospel with either the heathens or the religious/self-righteous.

> 2 Corinthians 11:24–28: *"Five times I received from the Jews thirty-nine lashes. Three times I was beaten with rods, once I was stoned, three times I was shipwrecked, a night and a day I have spent in the deep. I have been on frequent journeys, in dangers from rivers, dangers from robbers, dangers from my countrymen, dangers from the Gentiles, dangers in the city, dangers in the wilderness, dangers on the sea, dangers among false brethren; I have been in labor and hardship, through many sleepless nights, in hunger and thirst, often without food, in cold and exposure. Apart from such external things, there is the daily pressure on me of concern for all the churches."*

I have encountered people who, when confronted with their sin, will want to argue about the *good things* they have done, as evidence that they are very *good people*. For example, in an attempt to dismiss his need for the gospel, a man may fondly reflect back on how he gave $5 to a beggar two weeks ago. It will not even cross his mind that God knows during the same week he lied 52 times, cheated on his taxes, hated the guy in the cubical next to him, lusted after a women in his office, watched a dirty movie, and used God's name in vain 173 times. When one's self-righteousness is under scrutiny, the person will either repent or attack you!

Jesus gave an example of this in the parable of the dragnet in Matthew 13:47-52. He taught about the kingdom of heaven, righteousness and the judgment of the wicked. He specifically stated that as for the wicked, God, *"will throw them into the furnace of fire; in that place there will be weeping and gnashing of teeth."* (v. 50). How did the self-righteous in the crowd respond to Jesus' parable? They did not smile and tell Him they appreciated His loving concern for their souls. No, scripture states that in His hometown *"... they took offense at Him...."* (Matthew 13:57). As time went on, the offense transformed into a homicidal conspiracy *"... and the chief priests and the scribes were seeking how to seize Him by stealth and kill Him...."* (Mark 14:1).

Jesus *promised* that as a true disciple of His, you too will receive persecution and slander.

> John 15:20: *"Remember the word that I said to you, 'A slave is not greater than his master.' If they persecuted Me, they will also persecute you; if they kept My word, they will keep yours also."*

This is why many exchange real evangelism for the fake commission. By attempting to market the gospel, you have a much better chance of not offending others. On the other hand, the effective Christian is more concerned with offending God than man. To learn how to effectively evangelize, we will start with our main text, Matthew 5:13-20:

> *"You are the salt of the earth; but if the salt has become tasteless, how will it be made salty again? It is good for nothing anymore, except to be thrown out and trampled under foot by men. 14 You are the light of the world. A city set on a hill cannot be hidden. 15 Nor do men light a lamp, and put it under the peck-measure, but on the lampstand; and it gives light to all who are in the house. 16 Let your light shine before men in such a way that they may see your good works, and glorify your Father who is in heaven. 17 Do not think that I came to abolish the Law or the Prophets; I did not come to abolish, but to fulfill. 18 For truly I say to you, until heaven and earth pass away, not the smallest letter or stroke shall pass away from the Law, until all is accomplished. 19 Whoever then annuls one of the least of these commandments, and so teaches others, shall be called least in the kingdom of heaven; but whoever keeps and*

teaches them, he shall be called great in the kingdom of heaven. [20] *For I say to you, that unless your righteousness surpasses that of the scribes and Pharisees, you shall not enter the kingdom of heaven."*

In this section of Matthew, we see that the Christian is to bring *light and truth* to a dark and deceived world. This occurs by the power of the Holy Spirit moving through the believer who then *proclaims the Truth* and *engages in good works* for the *glory of God*. To effectively proclaim the truth, we use the perfect Law of God (the Ten Commandments) to illuminate a person regarding his sinful state. If one is convicted by the Holy Spirit regarding his sinfulness, that person should be driven to Christ to escape the eternal judgment in hell.

Romans 7:5–8: *"For while we were in the flesh, the sinful passions, which were aroused by the Law, were at work in the members of our body to bear fruit for death. But now we have been released from the Law, having died to that by which we were bound, so that we serve in newness of the Spirit and not in oldness of the letter. What shall we say then? Is the Law sin? May it never be! On the contrary, I would not have come to know sin except through the Law; for I would not have known about coveting if the Law had not said, 'You shall not covet.' But sin, taking opportunity through the commandment, produced in me coveting of every kind; for apart from the Law sin is dead."*

Now we will breakdown Matthew 5:13-20 into smaller portions starting with:

VERSES 13-16: *"You are the salt of the earth; but if the salt has become tasteless, how will it be made salty again? It is good for nothing anymore, except to be thrown out and trampled under foot by men.* [14] *You are the light of the world. A city set on a hill cannot be hidden.* [15] *Nor do men light a lamp, and put it under the peck-measure, but on the lampstand; and it gives light to all who are in the house.* [16]*Let your light shine before men in such a way that they may see your good works, and glorify your Father who is in heaven."*

Those who think that over time humanity is "getting better and better" are unbiblical and naive at best.[91] Scripture says that some will go from *bad to worse* as time goes on: *"But evil men and impostors will proceed from bad to worse, deceiving and being deceived."* (2 Timothy 3:13). Salt is not merely used as a flavoring, but it is also used as a preservative. As Christians, we are to be people of influence. The idea of Christians being *"salt of the earth"* is that we serve as a preserving element to an otherwise degenerating and godless society. We are to have a Spirit-led impact on society and not just be *"tasteless."* Unfortunately, many Christians have forfeited their most effective form of being a preserving element, which is preaching the true gospel. It is the gospel alone which can transform a person from the kingdom of darkness to light. When the gospel is downplayed and the church emphasizes political and social agendas, it renders itself effective only on a surface level. Political and social agendas can at best bring only a *temporary reform*[92]...the gospel alone can bring *transformation* of the soul.

---

[91] 2 Timothy 3:1–5: *"But realize this, that in the last days difficult times will come. For men will be lovers of self, lovers of money, boastful, arrogant, revilers, disobedient to parents, ungrateful, unholy, unloving, irreconcilable, malicious gossips, without self-control, brutal, haters of good, treacherous, reckless, conceited, lovers of pleasure rather than lovers of God, holding to a form of godliness, although they have denied its power; Avoid such men as these."*

[92] I know some Christians get overly preoccupied with political issues. I am not advocating any disregard of the believer's responsibility in public discourse. Further, I am not naïve regarding such issues. From my experience serving as a college intern for a U.S. Senator in Washington, D.C., to having worked in many administrations of politically elected officials, I understand the seriousness of political issues in the molding of our society. In the same vein, there were plenty of political issues swirling around while Jesus was on earth (e.g. Roman control of Israel, factions of Sadducees and

Jesus said in John 9:5: *"While I am in the world, I am the light of the world."* Now that Jesus has left the world, His light shines through His people. Notice verse 14 says we are also the *"light of the world"* in that the Holy Spirit, which indwells us, leads the Christian to tell others of God's great plan of salvation. Ephesians 5:8-9 says, *"...for you were formerly darkness, but now you are light in the Lord; walk as children of light ⁹(for the fruit of the light consists in all goodness and righteousness and truth)...."* We cannot influence the world for God if we live like the world. Matthew 5:15 states that we are not to, *"...light a lamp, and put it under a basket...."* In the same way, we are not to take the truth regarding the way of salvation and "hide" it from the world. A person who hides the truth about Christ is typically ashamed of Him. Jesus said:

> *"Whosoever therefore shall be ashamed of me and of my words in this adulterous and sinful generation; of him also shall the Son of man be ashamed, when he cometh in the glory of his Father with the holy angels."* (Mark 8:38).

One last thought about Christian service: We are not to be like the unconverted who do their *good works* to get the attention and praise of others. As Christians, we are to do good works (Ephesians 2:10) for the glory of God, not for our glory. Also, whenever possible, we are to do our good works in secret (Matthew 6:1-4).

Since it is clear we are to be light to a fallen world, we can examine how the law of God is used to shine the light of the gospel into the eyes of the lost. Matthew 5:17-20 states:

Pharisees, etc.). We do not see Jesus setting up political action committees or leading insurrections. My point being, it is unfortunate when some in the church do not evangelize, but work feverishly on political issues. Some of these folks think nothing of investing large amounts of time and money into political candidates, yet they do not do the same when it comes to gospel evangelism.

"Do not think that I came to abolish the Law or the Prophets; I did not come to abolish, but to fulfill. [18]For truly I say to you, until heaven and earth pass away, not the smallest letter or stroke shall pass away from the Law, until all is accomplished. [19]Whoever then annuls one of the least of these commandments, and so teaches others, shall be called least in the kingdom of heaven; but whoever keeps and teaches them, he shall be called great in the kingdom of heaven. [20]For I say to you, that unless your righteousness surpasses that of the scribes and Pharisees, you shall not enter the kingdom of heaven."

Jesus said He did not come *"to abolish the Law,"* but to fulfill it. Some people think that the Old Testament Law is something bad. This is wrong thinking. The Bible says, *"So then, the Law is holy, and the commandment is holy and righteous and good."* (Roman 7:12). Jesus also said, *"But it is easier for heaven and earth to pass away than for one stroke of a letter of the Law to fail."* (Luke 16:17). (See also our main text in Matthew 5:18.)

When accurately sharing the gospel, there are some basic concepts to apply. The Christian should be prepared to have a conversation with the unsaved, and explain why he is a disciple of Christ (i.e. why he has the hope of eternal life): *"but sanctify Christ as Lord in your hearts, always being ready to make a defense to everyone who asks you to give an account for the hope that is in you, yet with gentleness and reverence."* (1 Peter 3:15).

You are not getting into a debate with the objective to crush and humiliate the person who is arguing with you (*with gentleness*). Gentleness does not mean you are cowering to keep from offending the person because the gospel is already an offense to the natural mind (1 Corinthians 2:14, Romans 9:32-33). Gentleness means that you understand the unbeliever is completely blind to the things of God (just as you were before Christ saved you!).

When 1 Peter 3:15 speaks of *reverence* (some translate as fear) it means that we are not to be arrogant and disrespectful to others, regardless of how they respond to us. Further, it does not mean we have a fear of man. Many verses speak against the fear of man and tell us instead to fear God. It is the fear of God in our life that is an important factor in drawing people to Christ: "*Therefore, knowing the fear of the Lord, we persuade men, but we are made manifest to God; and I hope that we are made manifest also in your consciences.*" (2 Corinthians 5:11). There are seven main concepts I believe are very important when sharing the gospel with the unbelievers:

> *First:* The person you are witnessing to must understand that failure to perfectly obey the law of God (in thought, word and deed) is sin. James 2:10: "*For whoever keeps the whole law and yet stumbles in one point, he has become guilty of all.*"

> *Second*: The person you are witnessing to must understand that to perfectly obey the law of God (in thought, word and deed) is absolutely impossible! Since no one can obey it completely, the law renders every person a guilty sinner. Romans 3:23: "*...for all have sinned and fall short of the glory of God....*" In summary, the law of God shows us God's standard of perfection to enter heaven, but by showing us that standard, it also shows us that we can never reach it. It is wrong to say the law is unfair or bad, just because we cannot perfectly keep it. Romans 7:7: "*What shall we say then? Is the Law sin? May it never be! On the contrary, I would not have come to know sin except through the Law; for I would not have known about coveting if the Law had not said, "YOU SHALL NOT COVET."* (See also 1 Timothy 1:8-11.)

> *Third*: The person you are witnessing to must understand that he will be judged by his deeds (i.e. whether he perfectly obeyed the law of God in thought, word and deed).

Revelation 20:11–15: *"Then I saw a great white throne and Him who sat upon it, from whose presence earth and heaven fled away, and no place was found for them. And I saw the dead, the great and the small, standing before the throne, and books were opened; and another book was opened, which is the book of life; and the dead were judged from the things which were written in the books, according to their deeds. And the sea gave up the dead which were in it, and death and Hades gave up the dead which were in them; and they were judged, every one of them according to their deeds. Then death and Hades were thrown into the lake of fire. This is the second death, the lake of fire. And if anyone's name was not found written in the book of life, he was thrown into the lake of fire."*

Fourth: The person you are witnessing to must understand the penalty for having sinned, even one time, is death and eternity in hell. James 1:15: *"...and when sin is accomplished, it brings forth death."* Revelation 20:14–15: *"Then death and Hades were thrown into the lake of fire. This is the second death, the lake of fire. And if anyone's name was not found written in the book of life, he was thrown into the lake of fire."* It must further be understood that the judgment is neither temporary, nor does it end in annihilation, so that you don't have to feel anything. The torment goes on and on...forever and ever. One-hundred million years is just the start in eternity. Examine and carefully consider the description of hell from God's Word.

[Flames and torment – Luke 16:19-31; Lake of fire which burns with brimstone - Revelation 19:20; Tormented day and night forever and ever in the Lake of fire - Revelation 20:10; Eternal fire...the blackness of darkness forever - Jude v.7, 13;

Everlasting destruction from the presence of the Lord - 2 Thessalonians 1:9; Where their worm does not die, and the fire is not quenched - Mark 9:43-48; Weeping and gnashing of teeth - Matthew 24:51; Everlasting punishment - Matthew 25:46; Indignation, wrath, tribulation and anguish - Romans 2:8,9; Shame and everlasting contempt - Daniel 12:2; Unquenchable fire - Luke 3:17.]

When the Holy Spirit grants understanding to a person that he is doomed to hell, this should cause him to run to Christ for forgiveness. Some will not, as they have hardened hearts. (Acts 19:8-9). Remember, success in evangelism is *not* getting someone to say a prayer, but to accurately explain the gospel, in love.

Fifth: The person you are witnessing to must understand the only way he will escape judgment for his sinful deeds is if someone else, who perfectly "fulfilled the Law," pays his death penalty for him. Jesus, as the divine Son of God, is the only One who perfectly fulfilled the law. (In Matthew 5:17 Jesus said He came to *"fulfill"* the Law.) Hebrews 4:15 explains that Jesus was *"...One who has been tempted in all things as we are, yet without sin."* So the same Law that shows us we are doomed to hell should also drive us to Jesus to be forgiven and have eternal life: *"Therefore the Law has become our tutor to lead us to Christ, that we may be justified by faith ...."* (Galatians 3:24).

Sixth: Make sure the person understands that he cannot *earn* forgiveness. He must understand that salvation has nothing to do with his righteousness, performing good works, engaging in a religious ceremony, or cleaning up his life. He is not going to heaven simply because at one time in his past he was baptized, confirmed, or said a prayer.

Seventh: You need to share the same message that Jesus preached: One must repent and believe the gospel. In Mark

1:14-15 it states that "... *Jesus came into Galilee, preaching the gospel of God,* *[15]and saying, 'The time is fulfilled, and the kingdom of God is at hand; repent and believe in the gospel.'*" Needless to say, it is the same message the Apostles preached (and so should we!) Acts 20:21: "*...solemnly testifying to both Jews and Greeks of repentance toward God and faith in our Lord Jesus Christ.*" The meaning of this was stated earlier in this book, but it is worth repeating:

- To *REPENT* means to turn from your sins and forsake them by the power of God.
- To *BELIEVE THE GOSPEL* means that one who is "born again" by the Spirit of God (John 3:3-8)[93] will:
  - Believe in Jesus Christ as Almighty God, who is without sin;
  - Believe in Jesus' sacrificial death on the cross as the only and complete payment for your sins;
  - Believe in Jesus' bodily resurrection from the dead on the third day;
  - Believe in Jesus as Lord over all things and confesses this fact to others.[94]

---

[93] The power of God – when one is born again. Note that the concept of "believing in Jesus" is more than simply agreeing with some facts about Jesus. Man is spiritually dead and it is an act of God that allows him to see the kingdom of God: "*Truly, truly, I say to you, unless one is born again he cannot see the kingdom of God.*" John chapter 3 is not an explanation on *how* to get born again; it is an explanation that it is a work of the Spirit of God. John 3:3–8: "*Jesus answered and said to him, "Truly, truly, I say to you, unless one is born again he cannot see the kingdom of God." Nicodemus said to Him, "How can a man be born when he is old? He cannot enter a second time into his mother's womb and be born, can he?" Jesus answered, "Truly, truly, I say to you, unless one is born of water and the Spirit he cannot enter into the kingdom of God. "That which is born of the flesh is flesh, and that which is born of the Spirit is spirit. "Do not be amazed that I said to you, 'You must be born again.' "The wind blows where it wishes and you hear the sound of it, but do not know where it comes from and where it is going; so is everyone who is born of the Spirit.*"

[94] For scriptural support of these concepts see the appendix at the end

Again, remember that successful evangelism is not measured by some outcome such as getting the person to say a prayer, etc. Success is measured by accurately sharing the truth of God by the power of the Holy Spirit.

Practical Application of the Law While Evangelizing

Over the decades I have used many different evangelism programs and methods. I have found that witnessing to people by using the Law of God (i.e. the Ten Commandments)[95] is a truly Biblical method. [For more in-depth instruction on evangelism using The Ten Commandments, see evangelist Ray Comfort's materials and his book *The School of Biblical Evangelism* (Bridge-Logos Publishers, 2004).] By using the Law of God to convict the conscience, the Christian is less tempted to pander to a cheap marketing/consumer view of the gospel. The marketing approach will make a subtle promise that the person who agrees to "accept Jesus" will be rewarded with a happy life, God will help fix all his problems and he will get heaven too!

Every disciple must understand that the true gospel is not appealing to the unbelieving world. We are not trying to get people to like us or *like* Jesus. The Law does not save people, but instead shows them their need for a Savior. As Warren Wiersbe

---

of this book entitled: *A GENERAL OUTLINE OF FUNDAMENTAL DOCTRINES OF CHRISTIANITY.* (Note: Romans 10:9: *"that if you confess with your mouth Jesus as Lord, and believe in your heart that God raised Him from the dead, you will be saved;"*)

[95] Much of the information listed has come from the excellent evangelism training for using the Law as taught by Ray Comfort. For instruction on evangelism using The Ten Commandments, see R. Comfort and K. Cameron, The School of Biblical Evangelism (Bridge-Logos Publishers, 2004.)

stated: "The law is not the gospel, but the gospel is not lawless."[96] Jesus said: *"If you love Me, you will keep My commandments."* (John 14:15).

Scripture tells us in 1 John 2:3-6 that:

> *"By this we know that we have come to know Him, if we keep His commandments. [4]The one who says, 'I have come to know Him,' and does not keep His commandments, is a liar, and the truth is not in him;[5] but whoever keeps His word, in him the love of God has truly been perfected. By this we know that we are in Him:[6] the one who says he abides in Him ought himself to walk in the same manner as He walked."*

Martin Luther points out that the Law reveals our condemned state so we see our need for Christ: "The first duty of a preacher...revealing of the law and of sin...."[97] In another work he further explained, "Thou are killed by the law, that through Christ thou mayest be quickened and restored to life."[98]

St. Augustine wrote:

> "Sin cannot be overcome without the grace of God, so the law was given to convert the soul by anxiety about its guilt, so that it might be ready to receive grace."[99]

---

[96] Wiersbe, W. W. (1996). *The Bible Exposition Commentary* (1 Timothy 1:1). Wheaton, Ill.: Victor Books.

[97] Martin Luther, *Letter of St. Paul to the Romans.* Translated by Bon Andrew Thomton, OS Bed Hans Volz and Heinz Blanke, Volume 2 p.iii.

[98] Martin Luther, *Commentary on Galatians*, p.212.

[99] Thomas C. Oden, *Ancient Christian Commentary on the Scriptures, Romans, Vol. VI*, p.182.

Charles Spurgeon explained why we should not avoid admonishing the lost regarding the law of God when he said:

> "By lowering the law you weaken its power in the hands of God as a convincer of sin. It is the looking glass, which shows us our spots, and that is the most powerful thing, though nothing, but the gospel can wash them away.... Lower the law and you dim the light by which man perceives his guilt. This is a very serious loss to the sinner rather than a gain."[100]

The Larger Catechism of the Westminster Confession Standards explains that:

> "The moral law is of use to unregenerate men, to awaken their consciences to flee from wrath to come, and to drive them to Christ; or, upon their continuance in the estate and way of sin, to leave them inexcusable, and under the curse thereof." [101]

Dr. D. Martin Lloyd-Jones stated the following regarding evangelism:

> "This doctrine [what sin is], therefore, is absolutely vital in determining our conception of true evangelism. There is no true evangelism without the doctrine of sin, and without an understanding of what sin is. I do not want to be unfair, but I say that a gospel which merely says, 'Come to Jesus,' and offers Him as a Friend, and

---

[100] Charles H. Spurgeon, *Metropolitan Tabernacle Pulpit, Vol. 28,* pp. 248, 285.

[101] Smith, M. H. (1996, c1990). *Larger Catechism of the Westminster Confession Standards;* Question 96. Index created by Christian Classics Foundation. (electronic ed.) Greenville: Greenville Presbyterian Theological Seminary Press.

offers a marvelous new life, without convicting of sin, is not New Testament evangelism. The essence of evangelism is to start by preaching the law; and it is because the law has not been preached that we have had so much superficial evangelism. Go through the ministry of our Lord Himself and you cannot but get the impression that at times, far from pressing people to follow Him and to decide for Him, He put great obstacles in their way. He said in effect: 'Do you realize what you are doing? Have you counted the cost? Do you realize where it may lead you? Do you know that it means denying yourself, taking up your cross daily and following Me?' True evangelism, I say, because of this doctrine of sin, must always start by preaching the law. This means we must explain that mankind is confronted by the holiness of God, by His demands, and also by the consequences of sin. It is the Son of God Himself who speaks about being cast into hell. If you do not like the doctrine of hell you are just disagreeing with Jesus Christ. He, the Son of God, believed in hell; and it is in His exposure to the true nature of sin that He teaches that sin ultimately lands men in hell. *So evangelism must start with the holiness of God, the sinfulness of man, the demands of the law, the punishment meted out by the law, and the eternal consequences of evil and wrongdoing.* It is only the man who is brought to see his guilt in this way who flies to Christ for deliverance and redemption. Any belief in the Lord Jesus Christ which is not based on that is not a true belief in Him. You can have a psychological belief even in the Lord Jesus Christ; but a true belief sees in Him one who delivers us from the curse of the law. True evangelism starts like that, and obviously is primarily a call to repentance, 'repentance toward God, and faith toward our Lord Jesus Christ.'" [102]

---

[102] Dr. D. Martin Lloyd-Jones, *Studies in the Sermon on the Mount.* (See his section on Matthew 5:27-30.)

But most important, the Word of God says:

> Psalm 19:7: *"The law of the LORD is perfect, converting the soul: the testimony of the LORD is sure, making wise the simple."*

In addition, the Law of God is the great equalizer. It does not matter whether a person is educated or uneducated, rich or poor or influential or uninfluential. The law leaves all people in the same place...guilty. I have seen business people talking seriously about the gospel with teenagers who confronted them with the law of God.

Let me explain this equalizer concept another way. Say you run into a proud graduate-biology student who is working on his doctorate. When he finds out you are a Christian, his pride will not let him give you the time of day. He wants to write you off as intellectually deficient for not being (like him) the highest form of life on the earth...an evolutionary/atheist. In reality, he is a weak man who loves his sin and would never give it up. Although he claims he is a man of science, in reality he is a man of *blind* faith who believes everything comes from...*nothing*. He claims to be even more sure that *nothing* did not come from someone named God! Perhaps he is one who claims there was a big bang.

Do not waste your time asking reasonable questions like, "Where did the matter come from at the time of the big bang?" Remember, you are not trying to convert an atheist into a theist. You are trying to share the gospel. You are trying to take a person who is heading to hell, to understand that he can be forgiven and escape the judgment to come. If you begin arguing with him about science, his ungodly pride, love of sin, and years invested in an education steeped in evolutionary philosophy, will never let him concede the argument. Instead of arguing about science, ask him if he is a good person. Even then his pride will cause him to defend his own righteousness—most people, deep in their hearts, understand that they are not innocent.

If you are able to walk him through the Law of God, you have taken him off his ivory tower of perceived intellectual superiority, and forced him to deal with his conscience. Thus the great equalizer! Almost everyone has a conscience that convicts us of the truth about ourselves and our sin.[103]

The point of using the law is to help the person understand that he is not as wonderful as he thinks he is. For example, if you ask the average person on the street if he is a good person, the typical answer is a confident, "Yes!" Most people like to grade themselves on the curve (i.e. comparing themselves to others). Scripture tells us that when one's righteousness is compared with the perfect law of God, the person's mouth is shut (i.e. he is prevented from claiming his own goodness and justifying himself).

Romans 3:19-20: *"Now we know that whatever the Law says, it speaks to those who are under the Law,*

---

[103] There are some who, because of their evil practices and hatred of God, have seared/callous consciences and have been turned over to a depraved mind.

o   1 Timothy 4:1–3: *"But the Spirit explicitly says that in later times some will fall away from the faith, paying attention to deceitful spirits and doctrines of demons, by means of the hypocrisy of liars seared in their own conscience as with a branding iron, men who forbid marriage and advocate abstaining from foods which God has created to be gratefully shared in by those who believe and know the truth."*

o   Ephesians 4:18–19: *"...being darkened in their understanding, excluded from the life of God because of the ignorance that is in them, because of the hardness of their heart; and they, having become callous, have given themselves over to sensuality for the practice of every kind of impurity with greediness."*

o   Romans 1:28–32: *"And just as they did not see fit to acknowledge God any longer, God gave them over to a depraved mind, to do those things which are not proper, being filled with all unrighteousness, wickedness, greed, evil; full of envy, murder, strife, deceit, malice; they are gossips, slanderers, haters of God, insolent, arrogant, boastful, inventors of evil, disobedient to parents, without understanding, untrustworthy, unloving, unmerciful; and although they know the ordinance of God, that those who practice such things are worthy of death, they not only do the same, but also give hearty approval to those who practice them."*

> *that every mouth may be closed, and all the world*
> *may become accountable to God;* [20]*because by the*
> *works of the Law no flesh will be justified in His*
> *sight; for through the Law comes the knowledge of*
> *sin."*

Ray Comfort provides a series of questions to ask the individual you are witnessing to. The following are some of those questions along with my slight paraphrases:

1. *Religious background or spirituality question:*

   You may start by asking the person, "Can I ask you an interesting question?" If he says yes, ask him, "Do you have a Christian background or consider yourself a spiritual person?" Regardless of the answer, you have the person thinking about spiritual things. If the person seems like he is willing to talk to you, go on to the next question. If not, ask him, "Did you get one of these?" Then hand him a quality gospel tract and wish him a good day.

2. *Are you a good person question:*

   If he seems willing to talk, ask the person if he considers himself a *good person*. Let him explain why he thinks he has done more good than bad, or how he tries to treat others like he wants to be treated. The person may go on to mention his charity work, service clubs, military sacrifice, church involvement, etc.

3. *Good-person test:*

   Ask him if you can put his claim of being a good person to a quick test.

   • Ask if he has ever heard of God's Ten Commandments.

   • Explain that the Ten Commandments are God's standard of righteousness. Then ask the person if he has obeyed all the commandments. Regardless of his answer say, "Let's look at what some of the Ten Commandments require."

A. One of the commandments is: *"Thou shalt not bear false witness...."*
   - Have you ever told a lie? What do you call someone who tells lies? So, what does that make you?
   - ❖ [Answer: A liar – Exodus 20:16.]

B. Another commandment is: *"Thou shalt not steal."*
   - Have you ever taken anything that did not belong to you? (Remember it does not matter if it was of small value, or took place a long time ago.) What do you call someone who has stolen? So, what does that make you?
   - ❖ [Answer: A thief – Exodus 20:15.]

C. Another commandment is: *"Thou shall not take the name of the Lord your God in vain."*
   - Have you ever used God's name in vain through swearing or saying "Oh my G_d!" Have you used Jesus' name as a curse word? The Bible says *"... for the Lord will not leave him unpunished who takes His name in vain."* Exodus 20:7.
   - If so, what does that make you?
   - ❖ [Answer: A blasphemer – Exodus 20:7.]

D. Another commandment is: *"Thou shall not commit adultery."*
   - Maybe you think you have not committed the act of adultery, but Jesus says the one who looks at another with lust has *"already committed adultery"* in his heart: Matthew 5:28. So, what does that make you?

❖ [Answer: At best, an adulterer at heart –
Exodus 20:14.]

E. Another commandment is: *"Thou shall not
murder."*
- Maybe you can claim to have not murdered
anyone, but have you ever hated anyone?
The Bible says that if you hate someone
you are a murderer! 1 John 3:15: *"Everyone
who hates his brother is a murderer; and you
know that no murderer has eternal life
abiding in him."*] So, what does that make
you?
❖ [Answer: At best, a murderer at heart,
Exodus 20:13.]

4. "Do you still think you are a good person"
question:
- Next explain that you have covered only five
of The Ten Commandments and there are five
more to go. Then ask him if he still thinks he
is a truly "good person" by God's standard,
which requires him to have perfectly obeyed
His Commandments (in thought, word and
deed) his entire life?

5. Innocent or Guilty question:
- Regardless of his answer, ask the person: "If
you died in the next five minutes would you
be judged as innocent or guilty based on The
Ten Commandments?"

6. Heaven or hell question:
- Do you think you would go to heaven or hell?
Let us look carefully at what the Bible states is
the punishment for those who have simply
told a lie: Revelation 21:8: *"… and all liars,*

their part will be in the lake that burns with fire and brimstone, which is the second death."

❖ **If the person says that he is going to heaven,** ask him why he thinks that. He may say things like, "I asked Jesus into my heart." Make sure he has truly repented of his sins and placed his faith in Jesus.

❖ **If the person says that he is going to hell,** ask him if he is concerned about that. I will often remind the person that eternity is not just another lifetime…it is forever and ever. Most people will say they are very concerned. It is at this point that I share that the Bible says there is nothing they can do to earn forgiveness, but God has made it available through Jesus Christ. I then tell them the gospel that Jesus preached: Mark 1:14-15: *"… Jesus came into Galilee, preaching the gospel of God, ¹⁵and saying, 'The time is fulfilled, and the kingdom of God is at hand; repent and believe in the gospel.'"*

- To *REPENT* means to turn from your sins and forsake them by the power of God.
- To *BELIEVE THE GOSPEL* means that one who is "born again" by the Spirit of God (John 3:3-8)[104] will:

---

[104] The power of God – when one is born again. Note that the concept of "believing in Jesus" is more than simply agreeing with some facts about Jesus. Man is spiritually dead and it is the act of God that allows him to see the kingdom of God: *"Truly, truly, I say to you, unless one is born again he cannot see the kingdom of God."* John chapter 3 is not an explanation on *how* to get born again; it is an explanation that it is a work of the Spirit of God. John 3:3–8: *"Jesus answered and said to him, "Truly, truly, I say to you, unless one is born again he cannot see the kingdom of God." Nicodemus said to Him, "How can a man be born when he is old? He cannot enter a second time into his mother's womb and be born, can he?" Jesus answered, "Truly, truly, I say to you, unless one is born of water and the Spirit he cannot enter into the kingdom of God. "That which is born of the flesh is flesh, and that which is born of the Spirit is spirit. "Do not be amazed that I said to you, 'You must be born again.' "The wind blows where it*

- Believe in Jesus Christ as Almighty God, who is without sin;
- Believe in Jesus' sacrificial death on the cross as the only and complete payment for your sins;
- Believe in Jesus' bodily resurrection from the dead on the third day;
- Believe in Jesus as Lord over all things and confesses this fact to others.[105]

There you have it. In a couple of minutes you have shared the true gospel, using the Law of God. Remember, you are not trying to get a commitment or a prayer from the person. What is your objective? You want to accurately share the truth in love by the power of the Holy Spirit. That's it. It is the Holy Spirit who can cause the conviction to bring one to salvation. Remember that Jesus said in Matthew 7:14: *"For the gate is small and the way is narrow that leads to life, and there are few who find it."*

The response to Christ's sacrifice and forgiveness is either acceptance or rejection. In <u>Hebrews 2:3</u> it states, *"how shall we escape if we neglect so great a salvation?...."* Many will neglect or even reject such salvation, even though there is no escape for them.

When you realize Jesus paid such a price that you could never pay, how does that impact your devotion to Him? There is

---

wishes and you hear the sound of it, but do not know where it comes from and where it is going; so is everyone who is born of the Spirit."

[105] For scriptural support of these concepts see the appendix at the end of this book entitled: *A GENERAL OUTLINE OF FUNDAMENTAL DOCTRINES OF CHRISTIANITY.* (Note: Romans 10:9: *"that if you confess with your mouth Jesus as Lord, and believe in your heart that God raised Him from the dead, you will be saved...."*)

no need to be proud of yourself when you actually obey the Great Commission. Instead, we are to have the attitude Jesus tell us:

> Luke 17:7–10: *"Which of you, having a slave plowing or tending sheep, will say to him when he has come in from the field, 'Come immediately and sit down to eat'? But will he not say to him, 'Prepare something for me to eat, and properly clothe yourself and serve me while I eat and drink; and afterward you may eat and drink'? He does not thank the slave because he did the things which were commanded, does he? So you too, when you do all the things which are commanded you, say, 'We are unworthy slaves; we have done only that which we ought to have done.'...."*

May the Lord of the Harvest bless your work in His field — to accomplish the Great Commission (Luke 10:2).

SUMMARY OF THIS BOOK

Two matters to always remember:

Nothing else matters but THE KING and HIS KINGDOM.
(cf. Matthew 13:44-46)
and
Apart from Jesus Christ, you can do nothing.
(cf. John 15:5)

One last matter addressing all that Jesus taught:
"If you know these things, you are blessed if you do them."
(John 13:17 — see context John 13:10-20)

APPENDIX

A GENERAL OUTLINE OF FUNDAMENTAL DOCTRINES OF CHRISTIANITY

True fundamental doctrines are derived from *Scripture alone* and do not originate from religious tradition or ecclesiastical groups or counsels. Oswald Chambers stated:

> "We are apt to forget that a man is not only committed to Jesus Christ for salvation; he is committed to Jesus Christ's view of God, of the world, of sin and of the devil, and this will mean that he must recognize the responsibility of being transformed by the renewing of his mind."[106]

A mature Christian is committed to the Bible to formulate his theological beliefs. From the study of Scripture, one will affirm the doctrines below. The list below forms a general outline of true Christianity:[107]

- **Inspiration, Inerrancy and Authority of Scripture:** Christ is the Word of God incarnate: John 1:1,14, 2 Peter 1:20-21, 2 Timothy 3:16, Proverbs 30:5-6, Revelation 22:18-19.

- **Virgin Birth:** Matthew 1:18-25, Luke 1:34-35, John 1:14.

---

[106] Chambers, O. (1993, c1935). *My utmost for His highest: Selections for the year* (September 9). Grand Rapids, MI: Discovery House Publishers.

[107] The outline is largely, but not exclusively from: MacArthur, J. (1994). *Reckless faith: When the church loses its will to discern.* p.102. Wheaton, Ill.: Crossway Books.

- **The Deity of Jesus Christ The Son of God:** He is God incarnate (God in a human flesh-and-blood body): Colossians 2:9, 1 John 5:20, Titus 2:13-14, John 8:58 and 10:30, Mark 14:61-62, John 20:28, Mark 15:39, John 21:14, Luke 22:70, John 20:31.

- **Jesus' Humanity:** His incarnation (1 John 4:2-3); He was tempted (Luke 4:1-13), hungry (Matthew 4:2), thirsty (John 19:28), slept (Matthew 8:24), died (Mark 15:39-45, Matthew 27:50).

- **Jesus' Sinlessness:** 2 Corinthians 5:21, Hebrews 4:15, 1 Peter 2:22, 1 John 3:5.

- **The Trinity:** Father, Son and Holy Spirit. There is one God who eternally exists in three persons. Each possesses the same nature and attributes but is distinct in office and activity: Deuteronomy 6:4, Matthew 28:19, John 10:30, John 17:21, John 10:38, 1 John 2:20-24. Jesus is the Son of God and Savior (John 20:31).

- **Jesus—Worker of Miracles, All-Powerful and Creator of All Things:** John 11:32-45, Matthew 12:22, Luke 7:21-23, Matthew 15:30-31, Mark 9:23, 10:27, Luke 1:37, 18:27; Creator of All Things: John 1:3, John 1:10, 1 Corinthians 8:6, Revelation 4:11, Genesis 1:1, Colossians 1:15-17, Hebrews 1:2.

- **Human Depravity:** Each person is morally corrupt and sinful which is the condition of being spiritually dead toward God: Romans 3:23, Ephesians 2:1-3, Ecclesiastes 7:20, Romans 5:12, Psalms 14:1-3, Romans 3:20, Psalms 143:2, Psalm 51:5.

- **Christ's Atoning Death and Bodily Resurrection:** Christ died on the cross as a substitutionary sacrifice for sinners: 1 Peter 3:18, 2 Corinthians 5:21, 1 Corinthians 15:1-7, Titus 2:13-14,

Romans 5:12-21, Hebrews 2:14, John 11:25-27, John 4:25-26, 1 John 2:1-2, John 21:14.

- **A Person is Saved from Eternal Damnation by God's Grace Through Faith in Jesus Christ and His Sacrificial Payment for Sin by His Death on The Cross (and nothing else):** One is not saved by works of righteousness, being a good person, or attempted obedience to the Law: Ephesians 2:8-10, Galatians 2:16 - 3:8, Romans 4:4-5, Romans 3:27-31, 5:11-21, Acts 10:43, Titus 2:13-14, John 3:15-18.

- **The Lordship of Christ:** Romans 10:9: *"that if you confess with your mouth Jesus as Lord, and believe in your heart that God raised Him from the dead, you will be saved;"* John 13:13: *"You call Me Teacher and Lord; and you are right, for so I am."* See also Philippians 2:8-11, 1 Corinthians 16:22-23, Romans 14:9, Acts 16:31, 1 Corinthians 12:3, Acts 2:21 and 36, Acts 1:21, Matthew 12:8, Matthew 22:37, Isaiah 45:23, Romans 14:11.

- **The Return of Christ:** Second Coming: John 14:1-3, Matthew 26:64, Luke 12:40, Matthew 24:27 and 42-51, Mark 14:62, John 21:21-23. Mark 13:26.

- **The Eternal Damnation in Hell for the Unsaved:** John 15:6, Revelation 20:10-15, Revelation 21:8, John 3:18, 1 Corinthians 6:9-11, 2 Thessalonians 1:8-9, John 5:22, Mark 9:43-48.

- **Eternal Reign Of Christ in Heaven and Eternal Life for those He Redeemed:** John 14:1-3, Matthew 19:28-29, Matthew 25:46, John 3:15-16, Revelation 4:5-11, 1 John 5:20, Jude v.21, 1 Peter 4:11, 1 John 1:2-4, Titus 2:13-14.

---

* Fundamental doctrines are those that are essential to one making a claim to true Biblical Christianity. What are the fundamentals of the faith? Most restrict the list of fundamental doctrines to those that relate to the issue of salvation alone (soteriological — the theological doctrine of salvation in Christianity). "Historically, fundamentalism has been used to identify one holding to the five fundamentals of the faith adopted by the General Assembly of the Presbyterian Church in the U.S.A. in 1910. The five fundamentals were: the miracles of Christ, the virgin birth of Christ, the substitutionary atonement of Christ, the bodily resurrection of Christ, and the inspiration of Scripture. Fundamentalism has stood for the historic fundamentals of Christianity, particularly as developed in *The Fundamentals*. These were initially issued as twelve booklets edited by R. A. Torrey and A. C. Dixon." Enns, P. P. (1997, c1989). *The Moody Handbook of Theology* p. 613. Chicago, Ill.: Moody Press. The reason for limiting it to the doctrine of salvation is due to the awesome and wonderful simplicity of becoming a true Christian! Romans 10:9: *"...that if you confess with your mouth Jesus as Lord, and believe in your heart that God raised Him from the dead, you will be saved...."*

THE

FAKE

COMMISSION